The
Radical
Cross

Living the Passion of Christ

A.W. TOZER

WingSpread Publishers
Camp Hill, Pennsylvania

3825 Hartzdale Drive · Camp Hill, PA 17011
www.wingspreadpublishers.com

A division of Zur Ltd.

The Radical Cross: Living the Passion of Christ
ISBN: 1-60066-157-2
LOC Control Number: 2006924728
© 2005 by Zur Ltd.

Previously published by Christian Publications, Inc.
First Christian Publications Edition 2005
First WingSpread Publishers Edition 2006

CONTENTS

The Radical Cross

We often hear the phrase "the crux of the matter" or "the crux of a situation." The word *crux* comes from Latin and simply means "cross." Why has the word *crux* come to be associated with a critical juncture or point in time? Because the cross of Jesus Christ is truly the crux of history. Without the cross, history itself cannot be defined or corrected.

There is another word we often hear when we are in the throes of indescribable pain—the word *excruciating*. That, too, derives from Latin and means "out of the cross." Across time and human experience the cross has been the historical event that intersects time and space and speaks to the deepest hurts of the human heart.

But we live with more than pain and suffering. We also live with deep hungers within the human heart. These existentially gnaw at us with a desperate constancy. There are at least four such longings. The hunger for *truth*, as lies proliferate. The hunger for *love*, as we see hate ruling the day. The hunger for *justice*, as we see injustice mocking the law. The hunger for *forgiveness*, when we ourselves fail and stumble. These four stirrings grip the soul. As I see it, there is only one place in the world where these four hungers converge. That is at the cross. I dare say, therefore, that in this mix of pain and longing the divine answer is restoring and sublime. For within the paradox of the cross is the coalescing of our need and God's provision.

Some time ago, I spoke in Wales at an event that commemorated the 100th anniversary of the famous Welsh Revival of 1904. I listened many times to a magnificent hymn that was birthed during that revival, "Here Is Love." The melody is almost haunting, the words capturing the paradox of the cross. Here is one of the stanzas:

On the mount of crucifixion,
　Fountains opened deep and wide;
Through the floodgates of God's mercy
　Flowed a vast and gracious tide.
Grace and love, like mighty rivers,
　Poured incessant from above,
And heaven's peace and perfect justice
　Kissed a guilty world in love.

This is the paradox of the cross: Perfect peace and perfect justice became united in one death on a Friday afternoon some two thousand years ago. The thief who repented while hanging on the cross next to Jesus understood the paradox. No one else knew so well the physical agony of what Jesus was suffering in crucifixion. And the thief knew that he deserved it. He knew the fear of God. But he received the assurance of pardon from the blameless Man hanging beside him.

A.W. Tozer has been one of the greatest writers of all time on themes as profound as the soul's hungers. He well grasped the paradox of the cross. In his opening essay, "The Cross Is a Radical Thing," he exhorts the believer to resist the downgrading of the cross to a mere symbol. If the cross has become to us a humdrum ornament to our faith, we have not understood it, and we have not felt its offense.

Tozer's essays are truly needed in our day because he understood the death of Christ in both its timeliness and timelessness. The Apostle Paul captured this timelessness when he exhorted the Corinthian believers: "Whenever you eat this bread and drink this cup, you proclaim the Lord's death until he comes" (1 Corinthians 11:26). All the tenses were captured there—the present, the past and the future. The moment Christ died was an actual point in time in the past. He presently offers to live within us and promised to return.

Combined with the tenses are our tensions. Many of our modern-day sensibilities are offended by the brutality of a Roman crucifixion, and some people have even become persuaded that the atonement is a remote and irrelevant doctrine. Even so, the unprecedented violence occurring all over the world daily testifies to the greatest barbarism of all—the crucifixion of Christ—and to its message to the human race. I would go so far as to say that until we see the price God paid for our peace in His own Son, we will be paying with our sons' and daughters' lives on the battlefields of our hates and brutalities, only to find peace ever eluding us.

Never has it been more obvious that this world needs redemption, and that redemption is costly. The cross more than ever, in our language and in our longings, is necessary to bridge the divide between God and us. Without the cross the chasm that separates us all from truth, love, justice and forgiveness can never be crossed. The depths of mystery and love found in the cross can never be fully plumbed, but it must be the lifelong pursuit of the Christian to marvel at its costliness and to celebrate its meaning. That is why I commend these essays to you. Your understanding of the cross and your commitment to its imperative will be greatly increased. There is no more important theme than this one. It stands as the defining counter-perspective to everything this world has to offer. As you meditate upon this paradox that propels wonder and worship, may you be moved to sing with the hymn writer:

> Were the whole realm of nature mine,
>   That were a present far too small.
> Love so amazing, so divine,
>   Demands my soul, my life, my all!

Dr. Ravi Zacharias, President
Ravi Zacharias International Ministries
Atlanta, Georgia

PREFACE

O f the many compilations of Tozer's writings (there are now more than fifty titles available) this is the first collection to focus specifically on what he had to say about the cross of Jesus Christ. If there is one message that Tozer consistently preached with passion, it was the crucified life. Certainly, one of Tozer's most frequently used verses was Luke 9:23: "If anyone would come after me, he must deny himself and take up his cross daily and follow me."

For some 2,000 years, this message of the cross has stood as the chafing point between the physical and spiritual realms, between human and divine wills. The message of the cross is an agitant thrown into the mix of each new generation of every nation, creating conflict while at the same time offering true peace. Societies, including our own, will come and go. Nations will rise and fall. But the message of the cross will withstand all of its opposition through the centuries and emerge victorious with its triumphant King! That is why this is such an important book.

Much of Tozer's theology was informed by an intimate understanding of Dr. A.B. Simpson, who founded The Christian and Missionary Alliance movement in the late 1800s. In fact, one of Tozer's lesser known books, *Wingspread,* is a biographical account of the life of Albert B. Simpson.

Because of Tozer's affinity to Simpson, we have decided to include one of Simpson's messages in the Appendix at the end of this book. Simpson's writing (he wrote more than 100 books) is saturated with Scripture, and one gets the sense at times that his deep understanding of the Word may have come to him as direct revelations from the mouth of the Lord Himself.

Lastly, one cannot read this collection of essays without being personally convicted. It's not enough to admire Tozer's biblical insights and incisive commentary. Tozer would cringe at that. He would want you and me to become more like Christ as a result of reading these works.

What I appreciate most about Tozer's writings is that the more he came to understand what Christ accomplished on Calvary, the more he expressed utter amazement at the price God paid to redeem mankind. For all of his personal study of the mystics of old, Tozer was continually mystified by the atonement.

Though highly respected and a much sought-after speaker, though very confrontational and candid in his pulpit, Tozer knew all too well his lowly and meek position before the Almighty God. Perhaps, after all, that is where he derived his power to communicate so effectively.

I suppose that is the great lesson of this book: If we would be empowered for life and ministry, it will only happen as we are on our knees at the foot of the cross.

Douglas B. Wicks, Publisher
January 2005

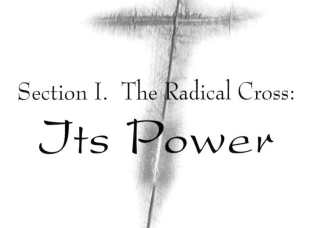

Section I. The Radical Cross:
Its Power

CHAPTER 1

The Cross Is a Radical Thing

T he cross of Christ is the most revolutionary thing ever to appear among men. The cross of old Roman times knew no compromise; it never made concessions. It won all its arguments by killing its opponent and silencing him for good. It spared not Christ, but slew Him the same as the rest. He was alive when they hung Him on that cross and completely dead when they took Him down six hours later. That was the cross the first time it appeared in Christian history.

After Christ was risen from the dead the apostles went out to preach His message, and what they preached was the cross. And wherever they went into the wide world they carried the cross, and the same revolutionary power went with them. The radical message of the cross transformed Saul of Tarsus and changed him from a persecutor of Christians to a tender believer and an apostle of the faith. Its power changed bad men into good ones. It shook off the long bondage of paganism and altered completely the whole moral and mental outlook of the Western world.

All this it did and continued to do as long as it was permitted to remain what it had been originally—a cross. Its power departed when it was changed from a thing of death to a thing of beauty. When men made of it a symbol, hung it around their necks as an ornament or made its outline before their faces as a magic sign to ward off evil, then it became at best a weak emblem, at worst a positive fetish. As such it is revered today by millions who know absolutely nothing about its power.

The cross effects its ends by destroying one established pattern, the victim's, and creating another pattern, its own. Thus it always has its way. It wins by defeating its opponent and imposing its will upon him. It always dominates. It never compromises, never dickers nor confers, never surrenders a point for the sake of peace. It cares not for peace; it cares only to end its opposition as fast as possible.

With perfect knowledge of all this Christ said, "If anyone would come after me, he must deny himself and take up his cross and follow me" (Matthew 16:24). So the cross not only brings Christ's life to an end, it ends also the first life, the old life, of every one of His true followers. It destroys the old pattern, the Adam pattern, in the believer's life, and brings it to an end. Then the God who raised Christ from the dead raises the believer and a new life begins.

This, and nothing less, is true Christianity, though we cannot but recognize the sharp divergence of this conception from that held by the rank and file of evangelicals today. But we dare not qualify our position. The cross stands high above the opinions of men and to that cross all opinions must come at last for judgment. A shallow and worldly leadership would modify the cross to please the entertainment-mad saintlings who will have their fun even within the very sanctuary; but to do so is to court spiritual disaster and risk the anger of the Lamb turned Lion.

We must do something about the cross, and one of two things only we can do—flee it or die upon it. And if we should be so foolhardy as to flee, we shall by that act put away the faith of our fathers and make of Christianity something other than it is. Then we shall have left only the empty language of salvation; the power will depart with our departure from the true cross.

If we are wise we will do what Jesus did: endure the cross and despise its shame for the joy that is set before us. To do this is to submit the whole pattern of our lives to be destroyed and built again in the power of an endless life. And we shall find that it is more than poetry, more than sweet hymnody and elevated feeling. The cross will cut into our lives where it hurts worst, sparing neither us nor our carefully cultivated reputations. It will defeat us and bring our selfish lives to an end. Only then can we rise in fullness of life to establish a pattern of living wholly new and free and full of good works.

The changed attitude toward the cross that we see in modern orthodoxy proves not that God has changed, nor that Christ has eased up on His demand that we carry the cross; it means rather that current Christianity has moved away from the standards of the New Testament. So far have we moved indeed that it may take nothing short of a new reformation to restore the cross to its right place in the theology and life of the Church.

CHAPTER 2

The Passion of Christ

The word *passion* now means "sex lust," but back in the early days it meant deep, terrible suffering. That is why they call Good Friday "Passion Tide" and we talk about "the passion of Christ." It is the suffering Jesus did as He made His priestly offering with His own blood for us.

Jesus Christ is God, and all I've said about God describes Christ. He is unitary. He has taken on Himself the nature of man, but God the Eternal Word, who was before man and who created man, is a unitary being and there is no dividing of His substance. And so that Holy One suffered, and His suffering in His own blood for us was three things. It was infinite, almighty and perfect.

Infinite means without bound and without limit, shoreless, bottomless, topless forever and ever, without any possible measure or limitation. And so the suffering of Jesus and the atonement He made on that cross under that darkening sky was infinite in its power.

It was not only infinite but *almighty*. It's possible for good men to "almost" do something or to "almost" be something. That is the fix people get in because they are people. But Almighty God is never "almost" anything. God is always exactly what He is. He is the Almighty One. Isaac Watts said about His dying on the cross, "God the mighty Maker died for man the creature's sin." And when God the Almighty Maker died, all the power there is was in that atonement. You never can overstate the efficaciousness of the atonement. You never can exaggerate the power of the cross.

And God is not only infinite and almighty but *perfect*. The atonement in Jesus Christ's blood is perfect; there isn't anything that can be added to it. It is spotless, impeccable, flawless. It is perfect as God is perfect. So Anselm's* question, "How dost Thou spare the wicked if Thou art just?" is answered from the effect of Christ's passion. That holy suffering there on the cross and that resurrection from the dead cancels our sins and abrogates our sentence.

Where and how did we get that sentence? We got it by the application of justice to a moral situation. No matter how nice and refined and lovely you think you are, you are a moral situation—you have been, you still are, you will be. And when God confronted you, God's justice confronted a moral situation and found you unequal, found inequity, found iniquity.

Because He found iniquity there, God sentenced you to die. Everybody has been or is under the sentence of death. I wonder how people can be so jolly under the sentence of death. "The soul who sins is the one who will die" (Ezekiel 18:20). When justice confronts a moral situation in a man, woman, young person or anybody morally responsible, then either it justifies or condemns that person. That's how we got that sentence.

Let me point out that when God in His justice sentences the sinner to die, He does not quarrel with the mercy of God; He does not quarrel with the kindness of God; He does not quarrel with His compassion or pity, for they are all attributes of a unitary God, and they cannot quarrel with each other. All the attributes of God concur in a man's death sentence. The very angels in heaven cried out and said,

> "You are just in these judgments,
>   you who are and who were, the Holy One,

---

* Anselm (1033-1109), a Benedictine monk, became a great philosopher and theologian of his day.

because you have so judged; . . ."
"Yes, Lord God Almighty,
    true and just are your judgments."
      (Revelation 16:5, 7)

You'll never find in heaven a group of holy beings finding fault with the way God conducts His foreign policy. God Almighty is conducting His world, and every moral creature says, "True and just are your judgments. . . . Righteousness and justice are the foundation of your throne" (Revelation 16:7, Psalm 89:14). When God sends a man to die, mercy and pity and compassion and wisdom and power concur—everything that's intelligent in God concurs in the sentence.

But oh, the mystery and wonder of the atonement! The soul that avails itself of that atonement, that throws itself out on that atonement, the moral situation has changed. God has not changed! Jesus Christ did not die to change God; Jesus Christ died to change a moral situation. When God's justice confronts an unprotected sinner that justice sentences him to die. And all of God concurs in the sentence! But when Christ, who is God, went onto the tree and died there in infinite agony, in a plethora of suffering, this great God suffered more than they suffer in hell. He suffered all that they could suffer in hell. He suffered with the agony of God, for everything that God does, He does with all that He is. When God suffered for you, my friend, God suffered to change your moral situation.

The man who throws himself on the mercy of God has had the moral situation changed. God doesn't say, "Well, we'll excuse this fellow. He's made his decision, and we'll forgive him. He's gone into the prayer room, so we'll pardon him. He's going to join the church; we'll overlook his sin." No! When God looks at an atoned-for sinner He doesn't see the same moral situation that He sees when He looks at a sinner who still loves his sin. When God looks at a sinner who still loves his sin and rejects the mystery of the atonement, justice condemns him to die. When God looks at a sinner who has accepted the blood of the everlasting covenant, justice sentences him to live. And God is just in doing both things.

When God justifies a sinner everything in God is on the sinner's side. All the attributes of God are on the sinner's side. It isn't that mercy is pleading for the sinner and justice is trying to beat him to death, as we preachers sometimes make it sound. All of God does all that God does. When God looks at a sinner and sees him there unatoned for (he won't accept the atonement; he thinks it doesn't apply to him), the moral situation is such that justice says he must die. And when God looks at the atoned-for sinner, who in faith knows he's atoned for and has accepted it, justice says he must live! The unjust sinner can no more go to heaven than the justified sinner can go to hell. Oh friends, why are we so still? Why are we so quiet? We ought to rejoice and thank God with all our might!

I say it again: Justice is on the side of the returning sinner. First John 1:9 says, "If we confess our sins, he is faithful and just and will forgive us our sins and purify us from all unrighteousness." Justice is over on our side now because the mystery of the agony of God on the cross has changed our moral situation. So justice looks and sees equality, not inequity, and we are justified. That's what justification means.

Do I believe in justification by faith? Oh, my brother, do I believe in it! David believed in it and wrote it into Psalm 32. It was later quoted by one of the prophets. It was picked up by Paul and written into Galatians and Romans. It was lost for awhile and relegated to the dust bin and then brought out again to the forefront and taught by Luther and the Moravians and the Wesleys and the Presbyterians. "Justification by faith"—we stand on it today.

When we talk about justification, it isn't just a text to manipulate. We ought to see who God is and see why these things are true. We're justified by faith because the agony of God on the cross changed the moral situation. We are that moral situation. It didn't change God at all. The idea that the cross wiped the angry scowl off the face of God and He began grudgingly to smile is a pagan concept and not Christian.

God is one. Not only is there only one God, but that one God is unitary, one with Himself, indivisible. And the mercy of God is simply God being merciful. And the justice of God is simply God being just. And the love of God is simply God loving. And the compassion of God is simply God being compassionate. It's not something that runs out of God—*it's something God is!*

CHAPTER 3

The Easter Emphasis

At the risk of sounding more than slightly repetitious, I want to urge again that we Christians look to our doctrinal emphases.

If we would know the power of truth we must emphasize it. Creedal truth is coal lying inert in the depths of the earth waiting release. Dig it out, shovel it into the combustion chamber of some huge engine, and the mighty energy that lay asleep for centuries will create light and heat and cause the machinery of a great factory to surge into productive action. The theory of coal never turned a wheel nor warmed a hearth. Power must be released to be made effective.

In the redemptive work of Christ three major epochs may be noted: His birth, His death and His subsequent elevation to the right hand of God. These are the three main pillars that uphold the temple of Christianity; upon them rest all the hopes of mankind, world without end. All else that He did takes its meaning from these three Godlike deeds.

It is imperative that we believe all these truths, but the big question is where to lay the emphasis. Which truth should, at a given time, receive the sharpest accent? We are exhorted to look unto Jesus, but where shall we look? Unto Jesus in the manger? on the cross? at the throne? These questions are far from academic. It is of great practical importance to us that we get the right answer.

Of course we must include in our total creed the manger, the cross and the throne. All that is symbolized by these three objects must be present to the gaze of faith; all is necessary to a proper understanding of the Christian evangel. No single tenet of our creed must be abandoned or even relaxed, for each is joined to the other by a living bond. But while all truth is to be at all times to be held inviolate, not every truth is to be at all times emphasized equally with every other. Our Lord indicated as much when He spoke of the faithful and wise steward who gave to his master's household "their food allowance at the proper time" (Luke 12:42).

Mary brought forth her firstborn Son and wrapped Him in swaddling clothes and laid Him in a manger. Wise men came to worship, shepherds wondered and angels chanted of peace and good will towards men. All taken together this scene is so chastely beautiful, so winsome, so tender, that the like of it is not found anywhere in the literature of the world. It is not hard to see why Christians have tended to place such emphasis upon the manger, the meek-eyed virgin and the Christ child. In certain Christian circles the major emphasis is made to fall upon the child in the manger. Why this is so is understandable, but the emphasis is nevertheless misplaced.

Christ was born that He might become a man and became a man that He might give His life as ransom for many. Neither the birth nor the dying were ends in themselves. As He was born to die, so did He die that He might atone, and rise that He might justify freely all who take refuge in Him. His birth and His death are history. His appearance at the mercy seat is not history past, but a present, continuing fact, to the instructed Christian the most glorious fact his trusting heart can entertain.

This Easter season might be a good time to get our emphases corrected. Let us remember that weakness lies at the manger, death at the cross and power at the throne. Our Christ is not in a manger. Indeed, New Testament theology nowhere presents the Christ child as an object of saving faith. The gospel that stops at the manger is another gospel and no good news at all.

The Church that still gathers around the manger can only be weak and misty-eyed, mistaking sentimentality for the power of the Holy Spirit.

As there is now no babe in the manger at Bethlehem so there is no man on the cross at Jerusalem. To worship the babe in the manger or the man on the cross is to reverse the redemptive processes of God and turn the clock back on His eternal purposes. Let the Church place its major emphasis upon the cross and there can be only pessimism, gloom and fruitless remorse. Let a sick man die hugging a crucifix and what have we there? Two dead men in a bed, neither of which can help the other.

The glory of the Christian faith is that the Christ who died for our sins rose again for our justification. We should joyfully remember His birth and gratefully muse on His dying, but the crown of all our hopes is with Him at the Father's right hand.

Paul gloried in the cross and refused to preach anything except Christ and Him crucified, but to him the cross stood for the whole redemptive work of Christ. In his epistles Paul writes of the Incarnation and the Crucifixion, yet he stops not at the manger or the cross but constantly sweeps our thoughts on to the Resurrection and upward to the ascension and the throne.

"All authority in heaven and on earth has been given to me" (Matthew 28:18), said our risen Lord before He went up on high, and the first Christians believed Him and went forth to share His triumph. "With great power the apostles continued to testify to the resurrection of the Lord Jesus, and much grace was upon them all" (Acts 4:33).

Should the Church shift her emphasis from the weakness of the manger and the death of the cross to the life and power of the enthroned Christ, perhaps she might recapture her lost glory. It is worth a try.

CHAPTER 4

What Is the "Deeper Life"?

It is becoming more evident every day that there has occurred in the United States over the past few years a positive movement toward a higher type of Christian life. Just when the various "holiness" churches have been reduced to virtual impotence and the bulk of Fundamentalism has sold its birthright for a mess of pottage, a counter movement has arisen within the body of contemporary Christian believers. Apparently this movement did not originate with any one man or woman or in any one place. Rather it is a spontaneous upspringing of spiritual desire among Christians of many and varying religious backgrounds. The movement is not organized—it has no local headquarters, no officers and no dues-paying members. So silently and mysteriously has its influence permeated modern evangelicalism that it can be likened to the action of the wind that "blows wherever it pleases" without earthly agency or previous human knowledge. Though the movement has no new doctrine or peculiar ideas, its members recognize each other wherever they meet and reach across denominational lines to clasp warm hands and whisper, "Brother!" "Sister!"

The growing interest in the deeper life on the part of rapidly increasing numbers of religious people is significant. The term itself is not new nor is it the property of any particular group or school of interpretation. The words, or something like them, have been used at various times in Church history to identify a revolt against the ordinary in Christian experience and the insatiable yearning of a few discontented souls after the deep, essentially spiritual and inward power of the Christian message.

The fact that so many professed Christians should be concerned with a "deeper life" is tacit evidence that their spiritual experience has not been satisfactory. Many have looked themselves over and have turned away disappointed. When they talked to other professed Christians, they discovered that others were no better off than themselves. Surely, they reasoned hopefully, there must be something better, sweeter, deeper than what they were experiencing day by day. So they have turned eagerly to the advocates of the deeper life and inquired earnestly, if a bit cautiously, just what they are talking about and where it is found in Holy Scriptures.

The deeper life must be understood to mean a life in the Spirit far in advance of the average and nearer to the New Testament norm. I do not know that the term is the best that could be chosen, but for want of a better one we shall continue to employ it. There are many scriptural phrases that embody the meaning we are attempting to convey, but *these have been interpreted downward and equated with the spiritual mediocrity now current. The consequence is that when they are used by the average Bible teacher today, they do not mean what they meant when they were first used by the inspired writers.* This is the penalty we pay for making the Word of God conform to our experience instead of bringing our experience up to the Word of God. When high scriptural terms are used to describe low spiritual living, then other and more definitive terms are needed. Only by using terms previously agreed upon and understood can there be true communication between teacher and learner. Hence this definition of the deeper life.

The deeper life has also been called the "victorious life," but I do not like that term. It appears to me that it focuses attention exclusively upon one feature of the Christian life, that of personal victory over sin, when actually this is just one aspect of the deeper life—an important one, to be sure, but only one. That life in the Spirit that is denoted by the term "deeper life" is far wider and richer than mere victory over sin, however vital that victory may be. It also includes the thought of the indwelling of Christ, acute God-consciousness, rapturous worship, separation from the world, the joyous surrender of everything to God, internal union with the Trinity, the practice of the presence of God, the communion of saints and prayer without ceasing.

To enter upon such a life, seekers must be ready to accept without question the New Testament as the one final authority on spiritual matters. They must be willing to make Christ the one supreme Lord and ruler in their lives. They must surrender their whole being to the destructive power of the cross, to die not only to their sins but to their righteousness as well as to everything in which they formerly prided themselves.

If this should seem like a heavy sacrifice for anyone to make, let it be remembered that Christ is Lord and can make any demands upon us that He chooses, even to the point of requiring that we deny ourselves and bear the cross daily. The mighty anointing of the Holy Spirit that follows will restore to the soul infinitely more than has been taken away. It is a hard way, but a glorious one. Those who have known the sweetness of it will never complain about what they have lost. They will be too well pleased with what they have gained.

CHAPTER 5

Crucified with Christ

I have been crucified with Christ and I no longer live, but Christ lives in me. The life I live in the body, I live by faith in the Son of God, who loved me and gave himself for me. (Galatians 2:20)

There seems to be a great throng of professing Christians in our churches today whose total and amazing testimony sounds about like this: "I am thankful for God's plan in sending Christ to the cross to save me from hell."

I am convinced that it is a cheap, low-grade and misleading kind of Christianity that impels people to rise and state: "Because of sin I was deeply in debt—and God sent His Son, who came and paid all my debts."

Of course believing Christian men and women are saved from the judgment of hell, and it is a reality that Christ our Redeemer has paid the whole slate of debt and sin that was against us.

But what does God say about His purpose in allowing Jesus to go to the cross and to the grave? What does God say about the meaning of death and resurrection for the Christian believer?

Surely we know the Bible well enough to be able to answer that: God's highest purpose in the redemption of sinful humanity was based in His hope that we would allow Him to reproduce the likeness of Jesus Christ in our once-sinful lives!

This is the reason why we should be concerned with this text—this testimony of the Apostle Paul in which he shares his own personal theology with the Galatian Christians who had become known for their backsliding. It is a beautiful miniature, shining forth as an unusual and sparkling gem, an entire commentary on the deeper Christian life and experience. We are not trying to take it out of its context by dealing with it alone. We are simply acknowledging the fact that the context is too broad to be dealt with in any one message.

It is the King James version of the Bible which quotes Paul: "I am crucified with Christ." Nearly every other version quotes Paul as speaking in a different tense: "I have been crucified with Christ," and that really is the meaning of it: "I have been crucified with Christ."

This verse is quoted sometimes by people who have simply memorized it and they would not be able to tell you what Paul was really trying to communicate. This is not a portion of Scripture which can be skipped through lightly. You cannot skim through and pass over this verse as many seem to be able to do with the Lord's Prayer and the 23rd Psalm.

The Full Meaning

This is a verse with such depth of meaning and spiritual potential for the Christian believer that we are obligated to seek its full meaning—so it can become practical and workable and livable in all of our lives in this present world.

It is plain in this text that Paul was forthright and frank in the matter of his own personal involvement in seeking and finding God's highest desires and provision for Christian experience and victory. He was not bashful about the implications of his own personality becoming involved with the claims of Jesus Christ.

Not only does he plainly testify, "I have been crucified," but within the immediate vicinity of these verses, he used the words I, myself and me a total of fourteen times. . . .

I believe Paul knew that there is a legitimate time and place for the use of the word *I*. In spiritual matters, some people seem to want to maintain a kind of anonymity, if possible. As far as they are concerned, someone else should take the first step. This often comes up in the manner of our praying, as well. Some Christians are so general and vague and uninvolved in their requests that God Himself is unable to answer. I refer to the man who will bow his head and pray: "Lord, bless the missionaries and all for whom we should pray. Amen."

It is as though Paul says to us here: "I am not ashamed to use myself as an example. I have been crucified with Christ. I am willing to be pinpointed."

Only Christianity recognizes why the person who is without God and without any spiritual perception gets in such deep trouble with his own ego. When he says *I*, he is talking about the sum of his own individual being, and if he does not really know who he is or what he is doing here, he is besieged in his personality with all kinds of questions and problems and uncertainties.

Most of the shallow psychology religions of the day try to deal with the problem of the ego by jockeying it around from one position to another, but Christianity deals with the problem of *I* by disposing of it with finality.

The Bible teaches that every unregenerated human being will continue to wrestle with the problems of his own natural ego and selfishness. His human nature dates back to Adam. But the Bible also teaches with joy and blessing that every individual may be born again, thus becoming a "new man" in Christ.

When Paul speaks in this text, "I have been crucified," he is saying that "my natural self has been crucified." That is why he can go on to say, "Yet I live"—for he has become another and a new person—"I live in Christ and Christ lives in me."

Section II. TheRadical Cross:
Its Price

CHAPTER 6

The Saint Must Walk Alone

Most of the world's great souls have been lonely. Loneliness seems to be one price the saint must pay for his saintliness.

In the morning of the world (or should we say, in that strange darkness that came soon after the dawn of man's creation) that pious soul, Enoch, walked with God and was not, for God took him; and while it is not stated in so many words, a fair inference is that Enoch walked a path quite apart from his contemporaries.

Another lonely man was Noah who, of all the antediluvians*, found grace in the sight of God; and every shred of evidence points to the aloneness of his life even while surrounded by his people.

Again, Abraham had Sarah and Lot, as well as many servants and herdsmen, but who can read his story and the apostolic comment upon it without sensing instantly that he was a man "whose soul was alike a star and dwelt apart"? As far as we know, not one word did God ever speak to him in the company of men. Facedown he communed with his God, and the innate

---

* antediluvians: individuals who lived in the period before the flood described in the Bible.

dignity of the man forbade that he assume this posture in the presence of others. How sweet and solemn was the scene that night of the sacrifice when he saw the lamps of fire moving between the pieces of offering. There alone with a horror of great darkness upon him he heard the voice of God and knew that he was a man marked for divine favor.

Moses also was a man apart. While yet attached to the court of Pharaoh he took long walks alone, and during one of these walks while far removed from the crowds he saw an Egyptian and a Hebrew fighting and came to the rescue of his countryman. After the resultant break with Egypt he dwelt in almost complete seclusion in the desert. There while he watched his sheep alone the wonder of the burning bush appeared to him, and later on the peak of Sinai he crouched alone to gaze in fascinated awe at the Presence, partly hidden, partly disclosed, within the cloud and fire.

The prophets of pre-Christian times differed widely from each other, but one mark they bore in common was their enforced loneliness. They loved their people and gloried in the religion of the fathers, but their loyalty to the God of Abraham, Isaac and Jacob and their zeal for the welfare of the nation of Israel drove them away from the crowd and into long periods of heaviness. "I am a stranger to my brothers, / an alien to my own mother's sons" (Psalm 69:8), cried one and unwittingly spoke for all the rest.

Most revealing of all is the sight of that One of whom Moses and all the prophets did write, treading His lonely way to the cross, His deep loneliness unrelieved by the presence of the multitudes.

> 'Tis midnight, and on Olive's brow
>   The star is dimmed that lately shone.
> 'Tis midnight; in the garden now
>   The suffering Savior prays alone.
> 'Tis midnight, and from all removed,
>   The Savior wrestles lone with fears;
> E'en that disciple whom He loved
>   Heeds not his Master's grief and tears.
>   —William B. Tappan

He died alone in the darkness, hidden from the sight of mortal man, and no one saw Him when He arose triumphant and walked out of the tomb, though many saw Him afterward and bore witness to what they saw.

There are some things too sacred for any eye but God's to look upon. The curiosity, the clamor, the well-meant but blundering effort to help can only hinder the waiting soul and make unlikely, if not impossible, the communication of the secret message of God to the worshiping heart.

Sometimes we react by a kind of religious reflex and repeat dutifully the proper words and phrases even though they fail to express our real feelings and lack the authenticity of personal experience. Right now is such a time. A certain conventional loyalty may lead some who hear this unfamiliar truth expressed for the first time to say brightly, "Oh, I am never lonely. God said, 'I will never leave you nor forsake you' (Joshua 1:5), and Christ said, 'Surely I am with you always' (Matthew 28:20). How can I be lonely when Jesus is with me?"

Now I do not want to reflect on the sincerity of any Christian soul, but this stock testimony is too neat to be real. It is obviously what the speaker thinks should be true rather than what he has proved to be true by the test of experience. This cheerful denial of loneliness proves only that the speaker has never walked with God without the support and encouragement afforded him by society. The sense of companionship which he mistakenly attributes to the presence of Christ may and probably does arise from the presence of friendly people. Always remember: You cannot carry a cross in company. Though a man were surrounded by a vast crowd, his cross is his alone and his carrying of it marks him as a man apart. Society has turned against him; otherwise he would have no cross. No one is a friend to the man with a cross. "Then everyone deserted him and fled" (Mark 14:50).

The pain of loneliness arises from the constitution of our nature. God made us for each other. The desire for human companionship is completely natural and right. The loneliness of the Christian results from his walk with God in an ungodly world, a walk that must often take him away from the fellowship of good Christians as well as from that of the unregenerate world. His God-given instincts cry out for companionship with others of his kind, others who can understand his longings, his aspirations, his absorption in the love of Christ; and because within his circle of friends there are so few who share his inner experiences he is forced to walk alone. The unsatisfied longings of the prophets for human understanding caused them to cry out in their complaint, and even our Lord Himself suffered in the same way.

The man who has passed on into the divine presence in actual inner experience will not find many who understand him. A certain amount of social fellowship will of course be his as he mingles with religious persons in the regular activities of the church, but true spiritual fellowship will be hard to find. But he should not expect things to be otherwise. After all, he is a stranger and a pilgrim, and the journey he takes is not on his feet but in his heart. He walks with God in the garden of his own soul—and who but God can walk there with him? He is of another spirit from the multitudes that tread the courts of the Lord's house. He has seen that of which they have only heard, and he walks among them somewhat as Zacharias walked after his return from the altar when the people whispered, "He has seen a vision" (see Luke 1:22).

The truly spiritual man is indeed something of an oddity. He lives not for himself but to promote the interests of Another. He seeks to persuade people to give all to his Lord and asks no portion or share for himself. He delights not to be honored but to see his Savior glorified in the eyes of men. His joy is to see his Lord promoted and himself neglected. He finds few who care to talk about that which is the supreme object of his interest, so he is often silent and preoccupied in the midst of noisy religious shoptalk. For this he earns the reputation of being dull and over serious, so he is avoided and the gulf between him and society widens. He searches for friends upon whose garments he can detect the smell of myrrh and aloes and cassia out of the ivory palaces (see Psalm 45:8), and finding few or none he, like Mary of old, keeps these things in his heart.

It is this very loneliness that throws him back upon God. "Though my father and mother forsake me, / the LORD will receive me" (Psalm 27:10). His inability to find human companionship drives him to seek in God what he can find nowhere else. He learns in inner solitude what he could not have learned in the crowd—that Christ is All in all, that He is made unto us wisdom, righteousness, sanctification and redemption, that in Him we have and possess life's *summum bonum.*[*]

Two things remain to be said. One, that the lonely man of whom we speak is not a haughty man, nor is he the holier-than-thou, austere saint so bitterly satirized in popular literature. He is likely to feel that he is the least of all men and is sure to blame himself for his very loneliness. He wants to share his feelings with others and to open his heart to some like-minded soul who will understand him, but the spiritual climate around him does not encourage it, so he remains silent and tells his griefs to God alone.

The second thing is that the lonely saint is not the withdrawn man who hardens himself against human suffering and spends his days contemplating the heavens. Just the opposite is true. His loneliness makes him sympathetic to the approach of the brokenhearted and the fallen and the sin-bruised. Because he is detached from the world he is all the more able to help it. Meister Eckehart[**] taught his followers that if they should find themselves in prayer, as it were, caught up to the third heavens, and happen to remember that a poor widow needed food, they should break off the prayer instantly and go care for the widow. "God will not suffer you to lose anything by it," he told them. "You can take up again in prayer where you left off and the

---

* *summum bonum*: a Latin phrase meaning the supreme good from which all others are derived.
**Meister Eckehart (~1260-1327): a German mystic.

Lord will make it up to you." This is typical of the great mystics and masters of the interior life from Paul to the present day.

The weakness of so many modern Christians is that they feel too much at home in the world. In their effort to achieve restful "adjustment" to unregenerate society they have lost their pilgrim character and become an essential part of the very moral order against which they are sent to protest. The world recognizes them and accepts them for what they are. And this is the saddest thing that can be said about them. They are not lonely, but neither are they saints.

CHAPTER 7

No One Wants to Die on a Cross

Jf we should suddenly be revealed to those around us on the outside as Almighty God sees us within our souls, we would become the most embarrassed people in the world. If that should happen, we would be revealed as people barely able to stand, people in rags, some too dirty to be decent, some with great open sores. Some would be revealed in such condition that they would be turned out of skid row. Do we think that we are actually keeping our spiritual poverty a secret, that God doesn't know us better than we know ourselves? But we will not tell Him, and we disguise our poverty of spirit and hide our inward state in order to preserve our reputation.

We also want to keep some authority for ourselves. We cannot agree that the final key to our lives should be turned over to Jesus Christ. Brethren, we want to have dual controls—let the Lord run it but keep a hand on the controls just in case the Lord should fail!

We are willing to join heartily in singing, "To God Be the Glory," but we are strangely ingenious in figuring out ways and means by which we keep some of the glory for ourselves. In this matter of perpetually seeking our own interests, we can only say that people who want to live for God often arrange to do very subtly what the worldly souls do crudely and openly.

A man who doesn't have enough imagination to invent any-thing will still figure out a way of seeking his own interests, and the amazing thing is that he will do it with the help of some pretext which will serve as a screen to keep him from see-ing the ugliness of his own behavior.

Yes, we have it among professing Christians—this strange in-genuity to seek our own interest under the guise of seeking the interests of God. I am not afraid to say what I fear—that there are thousands of people who are using the deeper life and Bible prophecy, foreign missions and physical healing for no other purpose than to promote their own private interests secretly. They continue to let their apparent interest in these things serve as a screen so that they don't have to take a look at how ugly they are on the inside.

So we talk a lot about the deeper life and spiritual victory and becoming dead to ourselves—but we stay very busy rescu-ing ourselves from the cross. That part of ourselves that we res-cue from the cross may be a very little part of us, but it is likely to be the seat of our spiritual troubles and our defeats.

No one wants to die on a cross—until he comes to the place where he is desperate for the highest will of God in serving Je-sus Christ. The Apostle Paul said, "I want to die on that cross and I want to know what it is to die there, because if I die with Him I will also know Him in a better resurrection" (see Philippians 3:10-11). Paul was not just saying, "He will raise me from the dead"—for everyone will be raised from the dead. He said, "I want a superior resurrection, a resurrection like Christ's." Paul was willing to be crucified with Christ, but in our day we want to die a piece at a time, so we can rescue little parts of ourselves from the cross. . . .

People will pray and ask God to be filled—but all the while there is that strange ingenuity, that contradiction within which prevents our wills from stirring to the point of letting God have His way. . . .

Those who live in this state of perpetual contradiction can-not be happy Christians. A man who is always on the cross, just piece after piece, cannot be happy in that process. But when that man takes his place on the cross with Jesus Christ once and for all, and commends his spirit to God, lets go of everything and ceases to defend himself—sure, he has died, but there is a resurrection that follows!

If we are willing to go this route of victory with Jesus Christ, we cannot continue to be mediocre Christians, stopped halfway to the peak. Until we give up our own interests, there will never be enough stirring within our beings to find His highest will.

CHAPTER 8

The Cross Does Interfere

Things have come to a pretty pass," said a famous Englishman testily, "when religion is permitted to interfere with our private lives."

To which we may reply that things have come to a worse pass when an intelligent man living in a Protestant country could make such a remark. Had this man never read the New Testament? Had he never heard of Stephen? or Paul? or Peter? Had he never thought about the millions who followed Christ cheerfully to violent death, sudden or lingering, because they *did* allow their religion to interfere with their private lives?

But we must leave this man to his conscience and his Judge and look into our own hearts. Maybe he but expressed openly what some of us feel secretly. Just how radically has our religion interfered with the neat pattern of our own lives? Perhaps we had better answer that question first.

I have long believed that a man who spurns the Christian faith outright is more respected before God and the heavenly powers than the man who pretends to religion but refuses to come under its total domination. The first is an overt enemy, the second a false friend. It is the latter who will be spewed out of the mouth of Christ; and the reason is not hard to understand.

One picture of a Christian is a man carrying a cross. "If anyone would come after me, he must deny himself and take up his cross daily and follow me" (Luke 9:23). The man with a cross no longer controls his destiny; he lost control when he picked up his cross. That cross immediately became to him an all-absorbing interest, an overwhelming interference. No matter what he may desire to do, there is but one thing he *can* do; that is, move on toward the place of crucifixion.

The man who will not tolerate interference is under no compulsion to follow Christ. "If anyone would," said our Lord, and thus freed every man and placed the Christian life in the realm of voluntary choice.

Yet no man can escape interference. Law, duty, hunger, accident, natural disasters, illness, death, all intrude into his plans, and in the long run there is nothing he can do about it. Long experience with the rude necessities of life has taught men that these interferences will be thrust upon them sooner or later, so they learn to make what terms they can with the inevitable. They learn how to stay within the narrow circular rabbit path where the least interference is to be found. The bolder ones may challenge the world, enlarge the circle somewhat and so increase the number of their problems, but no one invites trouble deliberately. Human nature is not built that way.

Truth is a glorious but hard mistress. She never consults, bargains or compromises. She cries from the top of the high places: "Choose my instruction instead of silver, / knowledge rather than choice gold" (Proverbs 8:10). After that, every man is on his own. He may accept or refuse, receive or set at naught as he pleases; and there will be no attempt at coercion, though the man's whole destiny is at stake.

Let a man become enamored of eternal wisdom and set his heart to win her and he takes on himself a full-time, all-engaging pursuit. Thereafter he will have room for little else. Thereafter his whole life will be filled with seekings and findings, self-repudiations, tough disciplines and daily dyings as he is being crucified unto the world and the world unto him.

Were this an unfallen world the path of truth would be a smooth and easy one. Had the nature of man not suffered a huge moral dislocation there would be no discord between the way of God and the way of man. I assume that in heaven the angels live through a thousand serene millenniums without feeling the slightest discord between their desires and the will of God. But not so among men on earth. Here the natural man receives not the things of the Spirit of God; the flesh lusts against the Spirit and the Spirit against the flesh, and these are contrary one to the other. In that contest there can be only one outcome. We must surrender and God must have His way. His glory and our eternal welfare require that it be so.

Another reason that our religion must interfere with our private lives is that we live in the world, the Bible name for human society. The regenerated man has been inwardly separated from society as Israel was separated from Egypt at the crossing of the Red Sea. The Christian is a man of heaven temporarily living on earth. Though in spirit divided from the race of fallen men he must yet in the flesh live among them. In many things he is like them, but in others he differs so radically from them that they cannot but see and resent it. From the days of Cain and Abel the man of earth has punished the man of heaven for being different. The long history of persecution and martyrdom confirms this.

But we must not get the impression that the Christian life is one continuous conflict, one unbroken irritating struggle against the world, the flesh and the devil. A thousand times no. The heart that learns to die with Christ soon knows the blessed experience of rising with Him, and all the world's persecutions cannot still the high note of holy joy that springs up in the soul that has become the dwelling place of the Holy Spirit.

CHAPTER 9

Chastisement and Cross Carrying

or the Christian, cross carrying and chastisement are alike but not identical. They differ in a number of important ways. The two ideas are usually considered to be the same and the words embodying the ideas are used interchangeably. There is, however, a sharp distinction between them. When we confuse them we are not thinking accurately; and when we do not think accurately about truth we lose some benefit that we might otherwise enjoy.

The cross and the rod occur close together in the Holy Scriptures, but they are not the same thing. The rod is imposed without the consent of the one who suffers it. The cross cannot be imposed by another. Even Christ bore the cross by His own free choice. He said of the life He poured out on the cross, "No one takes it from me, but I lay it down of my own accord" (John 10:18). He had every opportunity to escape the cross but He set His face like a flint to go to Jerusalem to die. The only compulsion He knew was the compulsion of love.

Chastisement is an act of God; cross carrying an act of the Christian. When God in love lays the rod to the back of His children, He does not ask permission. Chastisement for the believer is not voluntary except in the sense that he chooses the will of God with the knowledge that the will of God includes chastisement. "Endure hardship as discipline; God is treating

you as sons. For what son is not disciplined by his father?"
(Hebrews 12:7).

The cross never comes unsolicited; the rod always does. "If
anyone would come after me, he must deny himself and take
up his cross and follow me" (Matthew 16:24). Here is clear, intelligent choice, a choice that must be made by the individual
with determination and forethought. In the kingdom of God no
one ever stumbled onto a cross.

But what is the cross for the Christian? Obviously it is not
the wooden instrument the Romans used to execute the sentence of death upon persons guilty of capital crimes. The cross
is the suffering the Christian endures as a consequence of his
following Christ in perfect obedience. Christ chose the cross by
choosing the path that led to it; and it is so with His followers.
In the way of obedience stands the cross, and we take the cross
when we enter that way.

As the cross stands in the way of obedience, so chastisement
is found in the way of disobedience. God never chastens a per-
fectly obedient child. Consider the fathers of our flesh; they
never punished us for obedience, only for disobedience.

When we feel the sting of the rod we may be sure we are
temporarily out of the right way. Conversely, the pain of the
cross means that we are in the way. But the Father's love is not
more or less, wherever we may be. God chastens us not that He
may love us but because He loves us. In a well-ordered house a
disobedient child may expect punishment; in the household of
God no careless Christian can hope to escape it.

But how can we tell in a given situation whether our pain is
from the cross or the rod? Pain is pain from whatever source it
comes. Jonah in flight from the will of God suffered no worse
storm than did Paul in the center of God's will; the same wild
sea threatened the life of both. And Daniel in the lion's den was
in trouble as deep as was Jonah in the whale's belly. The nails
bit as deep into the hands of Christ dying for the sins of the
world as into the hands of the two thieves dying of their own
sins. How then may we distinguish the cross from the rod?

I think the answer is plain. When tribulation comes we have but to note whether it is imposed or chosen. "Blessed are you," said our Lord, "when people insult you, persecute you and falsely say all kinds of evil against you" (Matthew 5:11). But that is not all. Three other words He added: They are "because of me." These words show that the suffering must come voluntarily, that it must be chosen in the larger choice of Christ and righteousness. If the accusation men cry against us is true, no blessedness follows.

We delude ourselves when we try to turn our just punishments into a cross and rejoice over that for which we should rather repent. "But how is it to your credit if you receive a beating for doing wrong and endure it? But if you suffer for doing good and you endure it, this is commendable before God" (1 Peter 2:20). The cross is always in the way of righteousness. We feel the pain of the cross only when we suffer for Christ's sake by our own willing choice.

I think that there is also another kind of suffering, one that does not fall into either of the categories considered above. It comes neither from the rod nor from the cross, not being imposed as a moral corrective nor suffered as a result of our Christian life and testimony. It comes in the course of nature and arises from the many ills flesh is heir to. It visits all alike in a greater or lesser degree and would appear to have no clear spiritual significance. Its source may be fire, flood, bereavement, injuries, accidents, illness, old age, weariness or the upset conditions of the world generally. What are we to do about this?

Well, some great souls have managed to turn even these neutral afflictions to good. By prayer and self-abasement they wooed adversity to become their friend and made rough distress a teacher to instruct them in the heavenly arts. May we not emulate them?

Section III. The Radical Cross:
Its Purpose

CHAPTER 10

Christ Came for All People

For God did not send his Son into the world to condemn the world, but to save the world through him. (John 3:17)

W hen the Word says that God sent His Son into the world, it is not talking to us merely about the world as geography. It does not just indicate to us that God sent His Son into the Near East, that He sent Him to Bethlehem in Palestine.

He came to Bethlehem, certainly. He did come to that little land that lies between the seas. But this message does not have any geographical or astronomical meaning. It has nothing to do with kilometers and distances and continents and mountains and towns.

What it really means is that God sent His Son into the human race. When it speaks of the world here, it does not mean that God just loved our geography. It does not mean that God so loved the snow-capped mountains or the sun-kissed meadows or the flowing streams or the great peaks of the north.

God may love all of these. I think He does. You cannot read the book of Job or the Psalms without knowing that God is in love with the world He made.

He Came to People

But that is not the meaning in this passage. God sent His Son to the human race. He came to people. This is something we must never forget—Jesus Christ came to seek and to save people. Not just certain favored people. Not just certain kinds of people. Not just people in general.

We humans do have a tendency to use generic terms and general terms and pretty soon we become just scientific in our outlook. Let us cast that outlook aside and confess that God loved each of us in a special kind of way so that His Son came into and unto and upon the people of the world—and He even became one of those people!

If you could imagine yourself to be like Puck* and able to draw a ring around the earth in forty winks, just think of the kinds of people you would see all at once. You would see the crippled and the blind and the leprous. You would see the fat, the lean, the tall and the short. You would see the dirty and the clean. You would see some walking safely along the avenues with no fear of a policeman but you would see also those who skulk in back alleys and crawl through broken windows. You would see those who are healthy and you would see others twitching and twisting in the last agonies of death. You would see the ignorant and the illiterate as well as those gathered under the elms in some college town, nurturing deep dreams of great poems or plays or books to astonish and delight the world.

People! You would see the millions of people: people whose eyes slant differently from yours and people whose hair is not like your hair.

Their customs are not the same as yours, their habits are not the same. But they are all people. The thing is, their differences are all external. Their similarities are all within their natures. Their differences have to do with customs and habits. Their likeness has to do with nature.

---

* Puck: a mischievous imp from English folklore who was immortalized in William Shakespeare's *A Midsummer Night's Dream.*

Brethren, let us treasure this: God sent His Son to the people. He is the people's Savior. Jesus Christ came to give life and hope to people like your family and like mine.

The Savior of the world knows the true value and worth of every living soul. He pays no attention to status or human honor or class. Our Lord knows nothing about this status business that everyone talks about.

When Jesus came to this world, He never asked anyone, "What is your IQ?" He never asked people whether or not they were well traveled. Let us thank God that He sent Him—and that He came! Both of those things are true. They are not contradictory. God sent Him as Savior! Christ, the Son, came to seek and to save! He came because He was sent and He came because His great heart urged Him and compelled Him to come. Now, let's think about the mission on which He came. Do you know what I have been thinking about our situation as people, as humans?

Let us think and imagine ourselves back to the condition of paganism. Let us imagine that we have no Bible and no hymn book and that these 2,000 years of Christian teaching and tradition had never taken place. We are on our own, humanly speaking.

Suddenly, someone arrives with a proclamation: "God is sending His Son into the human race. He is coming!"

What would be the first thing that we would think of? What would our hearts and consciences tell us immediately? We would run for the trees and rocks and hide like Adam among the trees of the Garden.

What would be the logical mission upon which God would send His Son into the world? We know what our nature is and we know that God knows all about us and He is sending His Son to face us.

Why would the Son of God come to our race?

Our own hearts—sin and darkness and deception and moral disease—tell us what His mission should be. The sin we cannot deny tells us that He might have come to judge the world!

Why did the Holy Ghost bring this proclamation and word
from God that "God did not send his Son into the world to
condemn the world" (John 3:17)?

Men and women are condemned in their own hearts because
they know that if the Righteous One is coming, then we ought
to be sentenced.

But God had a greater and far more gracious purpose—He
came that sinful men might be saved. The loving mission of our
Lord Jesus Christ was not to condemn but to forgive and reclaim.

Why did He come to men and not to fallen angels? Well, I
have said this before in this pulpit, and I could be right although many seem to think that because others are not saying
it I must be wrong: I believe He came to men and not to angels
because man at the first was created in the image of God and
angels were not. I believe He came to fallen Adam's brood and
not to fallen devils because the fallen brood of Adam had once
borne the very image of God.

Morally Logical Decision

Thus, I believe it was a morally logical decision that when Jesus Christ became incarnate it was in the flesh and body of a
man because God had made man in His image.

I believe that although man was fallen and lost and on his
way to hell, he still had a capacity and potential that made the
Incarnation possible, so that God Almighty could pull up the
blankets of human flesh around His ears and become a Man to
walk among men.

There was nothing of like kind among angels and fallen creatures—so He came not to condemn but to reclaim and to restore and to regenerate.

We have been trying to think of this condescension of God
in personal and individual terms and what it should mean to
each one of us to be loved of God in this way.

Now I think I hear someone saying, "But John 3:16 does not
mention the cross. You have been telling about God's love but

you have not mentioned the cross and His death on our be-half!"

Just let me say that there are some who insist and imagine that whenever we preach we should just open our mouths and in one great big round paragraph include every bit of theology there is to preach.

John 3:16 does not mention the cross and I declare to you that God is not nearly as provincial as we humans are. He has revealed it all and has included it all and has said it all some-where in the Book, so that the cross stands out like a great, bright, shining pillar in the midst of the Scriptures.

We remember, too, that without the cross on which the Sav-ior died there could be no Scriptures, no revelation, no re-demptive message, nothing! But here He gave us a loving proclamation—He sent His Son; He gave His Son! Then later it develops that in giving His Son, He gave Him to die!

I have said that this must be a personal word for every man and every woman. Like a prodigal son in that most moving of all stories, each one of us must come to grips with our own per-sonal need and to decide and act as he did: "I am hungry. I will perish here. But I will get up. I will go to my father. I remember his house and his provision" (see Luke 15:17–20). He said, "I will go"—so he got up and went to his father.

You must think of yourself—for God sent His Son into the world to save you!

CHAPTER 11

Each His Own Cross

An earnest Christian woman sought help from Henry Suso* concerning her spiritual life. She had been imposing rigid austerities upon herself in an effort to feel the sufferings that Christ had felt on the cross. Things weren't going so well with her and Suso knew why.

The old saint wrote his spiritual daughter and reminded her that our Lord had not said, "If anyone would come after me, he must deny himself and take up *my* cross daily and follow me" (see Luke 9:23). He had said, "He must . . . take up *his* cross daily." There is a difference of only one small pronoun; but that difference is vast and important.

Crosses are all alike, but no two are identical. Never before nor since has there been a cross experience just like that endured by the Savior. The whole dreadful work of dying which Christ suffered was something unique in the experience of mankind. It had to be so if the cross was to mean life for the world. The sin bearing, the darkness, the rejection by the Father were agonies peculiar to the Person of the holy sacrifice. To claim any experience remotely like that of Christ would be more than an error; it would be sacrilege.

---

* Henry (Heinrich) Suso (~1296-1366): a German mystic born of a noble family, Henry Suso entered a Benedictine monastery at the age of thirteen. His "Book of Eternal Wisdom" became a popular book of meditations during the Middle Ages.

Every cross was and is an instrument of death, but no man could die on the cross of another; each man died on his own cross; hence Jesus said, "He must . . . take up *his* cross daily and follow me."

Now there is a real sense in which the cross of Christ embraces all crosses and the death of Christ encompasses all deaths. "We are convinced that one died for all, and therefore all died" (2 Corinthians 5:14). "I have been crucified with Christ" (Galatians 2:20). "The cross of our Lord Jesus Christ, through which the world has been crucified to me, and I to the world" (6:14). This is in the judicial working of God in redemption. The Christian as a member of the Body of Christ is crucified along with his divine Head. Before God every true believer is reckoned to have died when Christ died. All subsequent experience of personal crucifixion is based upon this identification with Christ on the cross.

But in the practical, everyday outworking of the believer's crucifixion his own cross is brought into play. "He must . . . take up *his* cross daily." That is obviously not the cross of Christ. Rather it is the believer's own personal cross by means of which the cross of Christ is made effective in slaying his evil nature and setting him free from its power.

The believer's own cross is one he has assumed voluntarily. Therein lies the difference between his cross and the cross on which Roman convicts died. They went to the cross against their will; he, because he chooses to do so. No Roman officer ever pointed to a cross and said, "If any man will, let him." Only Christ said that, and by so saying He placed the whole matter in the hands of the Christian. He can refuse to take his cross, or he can stoop and take it up and start for the dark hill. The difference between great sainthood and spiritual mediocrity depends upon which choice he makes.

To go along with Christ step by step and point by point in identical suffering of Roman crucifixion is not possible for any of us and certainly is not intended by our Lord. What He does intend is that each of us should count himself dead indeed with

Christ and then accept willingly whatever of self-denial, repentance, humility and humble sacrifice that may be found in the path of obedient daily living. That is *his* cross, and it is the only one the Lord has invited him to bear.

CHAPTER 12

Celebrating the Person of Christ

S ome think of Communion as a celebration—and in the very best sense it is. We gather to celebrate our Lord Jesus Christ. In order for us to grasp the spirit of this celebration, notice the relationship of Christ, the Son of Man, to five words with prepositions attached.

Devotion To

First, we celebrate Christ's "devotion to" His Father's will. Our Lord Jesus Christ had no secondary aims. His one passion in life was the fulfillment of His Father's will. Of no other human being can this be said in absolute terms. Others have been devoted to God, but never absolutely. Always there has been occasion to mourn the introduction, however brief, of some distraction. But Jesus was never distracted. Never once did He deviate from His Father's will. It was always before Him, and it was to this one thing that He was devoted.

Because it was not the Father's will that any should perish, Jesus was devoted to the rescue of fallen mankind—completely devoted to it. He did not do a dozen other things as avocations. He did that one thing that would permit a Holy God to forgive sin. He was devoted to the altar of sacrifice so that mankind might be rescued from the wages of sin.

One of the old Baptist missionary societies had as its symbol an ox quietly standing between a plow and an altar. Underneath was the legend: "Ready for either or for both!" Plow, if that be God's will. Die on the altar, if that be God's will. Plow awhile, and then die on the altar. I can think of no more perfect symbol of devotion to God.

That symbol certainly describes the attitude of our Lord Jesus Christ. He was ready first for His labors on earth, the work with the plow. And He was ready for the altar of sacrifice—the cross. With no side interests, He moved with steady purpose—almost with precision—toward the cross. He would not be distracted or turned aside. He was completely devoted to the cross, completely devoted to the rescue of mankind, because He was completely devoted to His Father's will.

Even "if we believe not," as the ancient hymn puts it (see 2 Timothy 2:13), Jesus' faithful devotion is unchanged. He has not changed. And He will not change. He is as devoted now as He was then. He came to earth to be a Devoted One, for the word *devoted* actually is a religious term referring usually to an animal, often a lamb, that was selected and marked for sacrifice to a god. So, our Lord Jesus Christ, the Lamb of God, was devoted—completely devoted—to be the Infinite Sacrifice for sin.

Separation From

The second phrase is "separation from." There are many ways in which our Lord deliberately separated Himself from those around Him. We might say He separated Himself from people for people. Jesus did not separate Himself from people because He was weary of them, or because He disliked them. Rather, it was because He loved them. It was a separation in order that He might do for them what they could not do for themselves. He was the only One who could rescue them.

Throughout history there have been those who have separated themselves from people for other reasons. Tymen of Athens turned sour on the human race and went up into the hills. He separated himself from mankind because he hated the human race. But the separation of Jesus Christ from people was the result of love. He separated Himself from them for them. It was for them He came—and died. It was for them that He arose and ascended. For them He intercedes at the right hand of God.

"Separation from" is a phrase that marked Jesus. He not only kept Himself separated from sinners in the sense that He did not partake of their sins, but He was separated from the snare of trivialities. We Christians do so many things that are not really bad; they are just trivial. They are unworthy of us—much as if we discovered Albert Einstein cutting out paper dolls.

Our minds may not be among the six greatest of the ages, but like Einstein's, our minds have endless capabilities. Our spirits were designed by God to communicate with Deity. Yet we consume our time in trivialities. Jesus was never so engaged. He escaped the snare of trivialities. He was separated from the vanities of the human race. Need I remind you in this context that if these words characterized Jesus, they must also characterize each of us who claims to be a follower of Jesus? The runner separates himself from street clothes in order to free himself for the race. The soldier separates himself from civilian garb in order to don equipment that helps his mission of combat. So we as God's loving disciples must separate ourselves from everything that hinders our devotion to God.

Three Other Phrases

I more quickly mention three other phrases in addition to these two. The third is "rejection by." Jesus suffered rejection by mankind because of His holiness. On the cross He suffered rejection by God the Father because He was ladened with our sins. He was vicariously sinful. "God made him who had no sin to be sin for us, so that in him we might become the righteousness of God" (2 Corinthians 5:21).

In that sense, Jesus suffered a twofold rejection. He was too holy to be received by sinful men. And in that awful moment of His sacrifice He was too sinful to be received by a holy God. So He hung between heaven and earth, rejected by both until He cried, "It is finished. . . . Father, into your hands I commit my spirit" (John 19:30; Luke 23:46). Then He was received by the Father.

But while He was bearing my sins—and yours—He was rejected by the Father. While He moved among men He was rejected by them because His holy life was a constant rebuke to them.

The fourth phrase is "identification with." Surely Jesus was identified with us. Everything He did was for us; He acted in our stead. He took our guilt. He gave us His righteousness. In all that Jesus did on earth, He acted for us because by His incarnation He identified Himself with the human race. In His death and resurrection He identified Himself with the redeemed human race.

As a blessed result, whatever He is we are. Where He is, potentially His people are. What He is, potentially His people are—only His deity excepted.

Finally, consider His "acceptance at." Jesus Christ, our Lord, has acceptance at the throne of God. Although once "rejected by," He is now "accepted at"! The bitter rejection has turned into joyous acceptance. And the same is true for His people. Through Him we died. Identified with Him, we live. And in our identification with Him we are accepted at the right hand of God the Father.

The Lord's table, the Communion, is more than a picture on a wall, more than a set of beads reminding us of Jesus Christ and His death. It is a celebration of His person—a celebration in which we gladly join because we do remember Him. By it we testify to each other and to the world of Jesus' sacrificial, conquering death—until He comes!

CHAPTER 13

The Old Cross and the New

A ll unannounced and mostly undetected there has come in modern times a new cross into popular evangelical circles. It is like the old cross, but different: the likenesses are superficial; the differences, fundamental.

From this new cross has sprung a new philosophy of the Christian life, and from that new philosophy has come a new evangelical technique—a new type of meeting and a new kind of preaching. This new evangelism employs the same language as the old, but its content is not the same and its emphasis not as before.

The old cross would have no association with the world. For Adam's proud flesh it meant the end of the journey. It carried into effect the sentence imposed by the law of Sinai. The new cross is not opposed to the human race; rather, it is a friendly pal and, if understood aright, it is the source of oceans of good clean fun and innocent enjoyment. It lets Adam live without interference. His life motivation is unchanged; he still lives for his own pleasure, only now he takes delight in singing choruses and watching religious movies instead of singing bawdy songs and drinking hard liquor. The accent is still on enjoyment, though the fun is now on a higher place morally if not intellectually.

The new cross encourages a new entirely different evangelistic approach. The evangelist does not demand abnegation of the old life before a new life can be received. He preaches not contrasts but similarities. He seeks to key into public interest by showing that Christianity makes no unpleasant demands; rather, it offers the same thing the world does, only on a higher level. Whatever the sin-mad world happens to be clamoring after at the moment is cleverly shown to be the very thing the gospel offers, only the religious product is better.

The new cross does not slay the sinner, it redirects him. It gears him into a cleaner and jollier way of living and saves his self-respect. To the self-assertive it says, "Come and assert yourself for Christ." To the egotist it says, "Come and do your boasting in the Lord." To the thrill seeker it says, "Come and enjoy the thrill of Christian fellowship." The Christian message is slanted in the direction of the current vogue in order to make it acceptable to the public.

The philosophy back of this kind of thing may be sincere but its sincerity does not save it from being false. It is false because it is blind. It misses completely the whole meaning of the cross.

The old cross is a symbol of death. It stands for the abrupt, violent end of a human being. The man in Roman times who took up his cross and started down the road had already said good-bye to his friends. He was not coming back. He was going out to have it ended. The cross made no compromise, modified nothing, spared nothing; it slew all of the man, completely and for good. It did not try to keep on good terms with its victim. It struck cruel and hard, and when it had finished its work, the man was no more.

The race of Adam is under death sentence. There is no commutation and no escape. God cannot approve any of the fruits of sin, however innocent they may appear or beautiful to the eyes of men. God salvages the individual by liquidating him and then raising him again to newness of life.

That evangelism which draws friendly parallels between the ways of God and the ways of men is false to the Bible and cruel to the souls of its hearers. The faith of Christ does not parallel the world, it intersects it. In coming to Christ we do not bring our old life up onto a higher place; we leave it at the cross. The kernel of wheat must fall into the ground and die.

We who preach the gospel must not think of ourselves as public relations agents sent to establish good will between Christ and the world. We must not imagine ourselves commissioned to make Christ acceptable to big business, the press, the world of sports or modern education. We are not diplomats but prophets, and our message is not a compromise but an ultimatum.

God offers life, but not an improved old life. The life He offers is life out of death. It stands always on the far side of the cross. Whoever would possess it must pass under the rod. He must repudiate himself and concur in God's just sentence against him.

What does this mean to the individual, the condemned man who would find life in Christ Jesus? How can this theology be translated into life? Simply, he must repent and believe. He must forsake his sins and then go on to forsake himself. Let him cover nothing, defend nothing, excuse nothing. Let him not seek to make terms with God, but let him bow his head before the stroke of God's stern displeasures and acknowledge himself worthy to die.

Having done this let him gaze with simple trust upon the risen Savior, and from Him will come life and rebirth and cleansing and power. The cross that ended the earthly life of Jesus now puts an end to the sinner; and the power that raised Christ from the dead now raises him to a new life along with Christ.

To any who may object to this or count it merely a narrow and private view of truth, let me say God has set His hallmark of approval upon this message from Paul's day to the present. Whether stated in these exact words or not, this has been the content of all preaching that has brought life and power to the world through the centuries. The mystics, the reformers, the revivalists have put their emphasis here, and signs and wonders and mighty operations of the Holy Ghost gave witness to God's approval.

Dare we, the heirs of such a legacy of power, tamper with the truth? Dare we with our stubby pencils erase the lines of the blueprint or alter the pattern shown us in the Mount? May God forbid. Let us preach the old cross and we will know the old power.

Section IV. The Radical Cross:
Its Pain

CHAPTER 14

Not Peace, But a Sword

It should always be kept in mind that the Church is a divine family and that its loyalties sometimes cut sharply across the ties that bind earthly families together.

The cross is a sword and often separates friends and divides households. The idea that Christ always brings peace and patches up differences is found nowhere in His own teachings. Quite the contrary is true. For a man to cast in his lot with Christ often means that he will be opposed by his blood relatives and will find his true family ties only in the community of regenerated souls.

Surely it is a most desirable thing to be reared in a Christian home. When a young man or woman is thus happily situated, conversion to Christ brings no rift to the family circle but rather seals and cements the earthly ties. We see sometimes whole families from the aged grandparents to the youngest child all joyously serving the Lord, and hardly anything under the sun could be more delightful. But it is not often so. More often the presence of a true Christian in the home, if it does not actually divide, does at least bring a serious divergence of interest and puts a real strain upon the solidarity of the household.

The weakness of much that passes for the Christian faith these days is seen in the readiness of many professed followers of Christ to make any concessions in order to "get along with people," especially with relatives and in-laws. The philosophy of mid-twentieth century Christianity is a philosophy of appeasement. Peace and unity have become the Castor and Pollux* of the majority of religious leaders, and truth is regularly sacrificed on their altars. The notion that "peace on earth" as the New Testament uses the words, means concord between light and darkness is foreign to the whole traditional Christian position. Our Lord cared nothing for the good will of bad men, nor would He alter one word of His message to stay in favor with anyone, be he Jew or pagan or even a member of His own earthly family. "For even his own brothers did not believe in him" (John 7:5).

No one has understood the meaning of the cross who puts blood ties alongside the ties of the Spirit. "Flesh gives birth to flesh, but the Spirit gives birth to spirit" (John 3:6). All fleshly relationships will be dissolved in the glory of the resurrection, including the relationship between husband and wife. For this reason our Lord said plainly that for some people it would be necessary to break family ties if they would follow Him.

> Do you think I came to bring peace on earth? No, I tell you, but division. From now on there will be five in one family divided against each other, three against two and two against three. They will be divided, father against son and son against father, mother against daughter and daughter against mother, mother-in-law against daughter-in-law and daughter-in-law against mother-in-law. (Luke 12:51–53)

> If anyone comes to me and does not hate his father and mother, his wife and children, his brothers and sisters—yes, even his own life—he cannot be my disciple. And anyone who does not carry his cross and follow me cannot be my disciple. (14:26-27)

---

* Castor and Pollux: twin brothers of classical mythology, especially honored by the Romans. Known as great warriors who were devoted to each other, Castor was a renowned horseman and Pollux a boxer.

What Christ is saying here is that faith in Him immediately introduces another and a higher loyalty into the life. He demands and must have first place. For the true disciple it is Christ before family, Christ before country, Christ before life itself. The flesh must always be sacrificed to the spirit and the heavenly placed ahead of the earthly, and that at any cost. When we take up the cross, we become expendable, along with all natural friendships and all previous loyalties, and Christ becomes all in all.

In these days of sweet and easy Christianity, it requires inward illumination to see this truth and real faith to accept it. We had better pray for both before time runs out on us.

CHAPTER 15

The Uses of Suffering

The Bible has a great deal to say about suffering and most of it is encouraging.

The prevailing religious mood is not favorable to the doctrine, but anything that gets as much space as the doctrine of suffering gets in the Scriptures should certainly receive careful and reverent attention from the sons of the new creation. We cannot afford to neglect it, for whether we understand it or not we are going to experience some suffering. As human beings we cannot escape it.

From the first cold shock that brings a howl of protest from the newborn infant down to the last anguished gasp of the aged man, pain and suffering dog our footsteps as we journey here below. It will pay us to learn what God says about it so that we may know how to act and what to expect when it comes.

Christianity embraces everything that touches the life of man and deals with it all effectively. Because suffering is a real part of human life, Christ Himself took part in the same and learned obedience by the things which He suffered. It is not possible that the afflicted saint should feel a stab of pain to which Christ is a stranger. Our Lord not only suffered once on earth, He suffers now along with His people. "Behold," cried the old saint as he watched a youthful martyr die, "Behold how our Lord suffers in the body of His handmaid."

> Think not thou canst sigh a sigh
>   And thy Maker is not by;
> Think not thou canst weep a tear
>   And thy Maker is not near.

There is a kind of suffering which profits no one: it is the bitter and defiant suffering of the lost. The man out of Christ may endure any degree of affliction without being any the wiser or the better for it. It is for him all a part of the tragic heritage of sin, a kind of earnest of the pains of hell. To such there is not much that we can say and for such there is little that we can do except to try in the name of Christ and our common humanity to reduce the suffering as much as we can. That much we owe to all the children of misfortune, whatever their color or race or creed.

As long as we remain in the body we shall be subject to a certain amount of that common suffering which we must share with all the sons of men—loss, bereavement, nameless heartaches, disappointments, partings, betrayals and griefs of a thousand sorts. This is the less profitable kind of suffering, but even this can be made to serve the followers of Christ. There is such a thing as consecrated griefs, sorrows that may be common to everyone but which take on a special character for the Christian when accepted intelligently and offered to God in loving submission. We should be watchful lest we lose any blessing which such suffering might bring.

But there is another kind of suffering, known only to the Christian: It is voluntary suffering deliberately and knowingly incurred for the sake of Christ. Such is a luxury, a treasure of fabulous value, a source of riches beyond the power of the mind to conceive. And it is rare as well as precious, for there are few in this decadent age who will of their own choice go down into this dark mine looking for jewels. But of our own choice it must be, for there is no other way to get down. God will not force us into this kind of suffering; He will not lay this cross upon us nor embarrass us with riches we do not want. Such riches are reserved for those who apply to serve in the legion unto the death, who volunteer to suffer for Christ's sake and who follow up their application with lives that challenge the devil and invite the fury of hell. Such as these have said good-bye to the world's toys; they have chosen to suffer affliction with the people of God; they have accepted toil and suffering as their earthly portion. The marks of the cross are upon them and they are known in heaven and hell.

But where are they? Has this breed of Christian died out of the earth? Have the saints of God joined the mad scramble for security? Has the cross become no more than a symbol, a bloodless and sterile relic of nobler times? Are we now afraid to suffer and unwilling to die? I hope not, but I wonder. And only God has the answer.

CHAPTER 16

Coddled or Crucified?

The spiritual giants of old would not take their religion the easy way nor offer unto God that which cost them nothing. They sought not comfort but holiness, and the pages of history are still wet with their blood and their tears.

We now live in softer times. Woe unto us, for we have become adept in the art of comforting ourselves without power.

Almost every radical effort of the Holy Spirit to lead us forth to heroic self-crucifixion is now tempered with a fine sophistry* drawn from—of all sources—the Word of God itself. I hear it often these days. The trick is to say, half comically, amused at our own former ignorance, "Once I was distressed over my lack of power, my spiritual sterility, as I then thought; but one day the Lord said to me, 'My child, etc., etc.' " Then follows a quotation direct from the mouth of the Lord condoning our weakness and self-coddling. Thus the very authority of divine inspiration is given to what is obviously but the defensive reasoning of our own hearts.

Those who will justify themselves in that kind of dodging are not likely to be much affected by anything I can say or write. No one is so dead as the man who has turned the very thunders of judgment into a lullaby to soothe him into sound sleep and

---

* sophistry: subtly deceptive reasoning or argumentation.

has made the sacred Scriptures themselves a hiding place from reality.

But to those who will hear I would say with all the urgency at my command: Though the cross of Christ has been beautified by the poet and the artist, the avid seeker after God is likely to find it the same savage implement of destruction it was in the days of old. The way of the cross is still the pain-wracked path to spiritual power and fruitfulness.

So do not seek to hide from it. Do not accept an easy way. Do not allow yourself to be patted to sleep in a comfortable church, void of power and barren of fruit. Do not paint the cross nor deck it with flowers. Take it for what it is, as it is, and you will find it the rugged way to death and life. Let it slay you utterly. Seek God. Seek to be holy and fear none of those things which you will suffer.

CHAPTER 17

Mortify the Flesh

Mortify therefore your members which are upon the earth; fornication, uncleanness, inordinate affection, evil concupiscence, and covetousness, which is idolatry. . . .

Servants, obey in all things your masters according to the flesh; not with eyeservice, as menpleasers; but in singleness of heart, fearing God. (Colossians 3:5, 22, KJV)

Christians might as well admit that there is a reality you have got to reckon with, and that is your flesh. By flesh, *I do not mean your body*. That old monastic idea that God is angry with your body is just as silly as it can possibly be. Your body is just the goat you ride around on, that is all. It is neither good nor bad; it is just your bones and flesh and blood, that is all. It is what the thinkers and the philosophers call amoral—not moral or immoral, just neutral.

So when the Bible says, "mortify your flesh," it does not mean kill your blood and your bones and your epidermis and your hair and teeth and eyes and stomach. God is not mad at our physical body. When the Bible says, "Mortify your flesh," it means your ego, your old man, that self, that evil that is in you. That birthday present you got from the devil when you were born. That inward thing. That is your flesh.

If the old man was something that could be lifted out, like an onion could be pulled out of a garden, then we'd all feel very proud of the fact that we'd been de-onionized and debunked. But the terrible part about crucifying the flesh is that the flesh is *you*. When the Lord says mortify the flesh, He doesn't mean abuse your body by starving it or lying on beds of nails. He means put yourself on the cross. That is what people do not want to do.

Some denominations started out believing in the doctrine of self-crucifixion, of putting ourselves to death, of mortifying the flesh through the cross of Jesus. That is all old stuff now; it belongs back there with the horse and buggy and high-button shoes. Nobody believes it anymore, or if they do, they do not live it. I think it is better not to believe it and say so, like some of our good Calvinist friends do, than to say you believe it and then live in spite of it, in defiance of it.

There are a lot of people trying to get away with the old man. What do I mean by the old man? I mean your pride, your bossiness, your nastiness, your temper, your mean disposition, your lustfulness and your quarrelsomeness. What do I mean, Reverend? I mean your study, your hunting for a bigger church, being dissatisfied with the offering and blaming the superintendent because you cannot get called. The reason you cannot get called is nobody wants you. That is what I mean, Reverend.

Deacons, what do I mean? I mean sitting around in board meetings wearing your poor pastor out because you are too stubborn to humble yourself and admit you are wrong.

What do I mean, musicians? I mean that demeanor that makes you hate somebody that can sing a little better than you can. I mean that jealousy that makes you want to play the violin when everybody knows you can't, especially the choir director. You hate him, wish he were dead and secretly pray that he would get called to Punxsutawney. That is what I mean. All of this may be under the guise of spirituality and we may have learned to put our head over on one side, fold our hands gently and put on a beatific smile like St. Francis of Assisi and still be just as carnal as they come.

I do not know why you fear sanctification and I do not care. But I do say this: You had better mortify your flesh, or your flesh will do something terrible to you. In these terrible days in which we live, we have not only accepted the flesh in its morally fine manifestation as being quite proper, but we have created an ignoble theology of "extenuating circumstances" by which we excuse the flesh.

People do not hesitate any more to say, "Oh, was I mad!" and then a minute later, lead in prayer. But he is just mumbling words. I have no confidence in a man who loses his temper. I do not believe that a man who blows up and loses his temper is a spiritual man, whether he is a preacher, a bishop or a pope. He is a carnal man and needs to be cleansed by fire and blood. But we have excused people who say, "I was mad." If you were mad, you were sinning and you need to be cleansed from your bad temper. But we have incorporated the flesh into our orthodoxy, and instead of being humble, we magnify the proud fellow.

Years ago God gave me an ice pick and said, "Now Son, among your other duties will be to puncture all the inflated egos you see. Go stick an ice pick in them." And there has been more popping and hissing in my ministry as the air goes out of egos. People hate me for that, but I love them for the privilege of whittling them down to size, because if there is anything that we ought to get straight, it is how little we are.

When I was a young fellow, I always loved guns. I had a .22 revolver and loved to shoot. Just for fun when I had nothing else to do, and that is rare now, I would go out shooting with another fellow, and we shot what we called a mud hen. It looked like a great big duck, but when we dressed it, it was the biggest hypocrite you ever saw. It was practically all feathers. It was not much bigger than an oversized robin when we got down to the real bird. That describes most Christians. We stand our feathers on end so people do not know how small we are.

The word *mortify* comes from the same Latin word as *mortuary*—a place where you put dead people. It means "to die." But we do not talk about that much any more. We talk about it, but we do not believe in getting reduced. But you will never be a spiritual man until God reduces you to your proper size.

Mortify is a New Testament word. Turn your back upon yourself and reckon yourself to be dead indeed and crucified with Christ. Then expect the blood of Christ and the power of the Holy Spirit to make real what your faith has reckoned. And then begin to live it. Some people go to an altar and get sanctified, but they're still resentful, they still have a chip on their shoulder. They still love money. They still have a temper. They still look where they should not. And then they claim to be sanctified. They are just pretenders, or worse than that, they are deceived persons. Either we mortify the flesh or the flesh will harm us to a point where we have no power, no joy, no fruit, no usefulness, no victory.

CHAPTER 18

The Cross of Obedience

Some people in reading the Bible say they cannot understand why Elijah and other men had such active power with the living God. It is quite simple. God heard Elijah because Elijah had heard God. God did according to the word of Elijah because Elijah had done according to the word of God. You cannot separate the two.

When we are willing to consider the active will of God for our lives, we come immediately to a personal knowledge of the cross because the will of God is the place of blessed, painful, fruitful trouble!

The Apostle Paul knew about that. He called it "the fellowship of Christ's sufferings." It is my conviction that one of the reasons we exhibit very little spiritual power is because we are unwilling to accept and experience the fellowship of the Savior's sufferings, which means acceptance of His cross.

How can we have and know the blessed intimacy of the Lord Jesus if we are unwilling to take the route which He has demonstrated? We do not have it because we refuse to relate the will of God to the cross.

All of the great saints have been acquainted with the cross—even those who lived before the time of Christ. They were acquainted with the cross in essence because their obedience brought it to them.

All Christians living in full obedience will experience the cross and find themselves exercised in spirit very frequently. If they know their own hearts, they will be prepared to wrestle with the cross when it comes.

Think of Jacob in the Old Testament and notice the direction from which his cross came—directly from his own carnal self. It took Jacob some time to discover the nature of his own heart and to admit and confess that Jacob's cross was Jacob himself.

Read again about Daniel and you will discover that his cross was the world. Consider Job and you will find that his cross was the devil. The devil crucified Job, the world crucified Daniel, and Jacob was crucified on the tree of his own Jacobness, his own carnality.

Study the lives of the apostles in the New Testament and you will find that their crosses came from the religious authorities.

Likewise in Church history we look at Luther and note that his cross came from the Roman Church which makes so much of wooden crosses, while Wesley's cross came from the Protestant Church. Continue to name the great souls who followed the will of God, and you will name the men and women of God who looked forward by faith, and their obedience invariably led them into places of blessed and painful and fruitful trouble.

I must point out here the fallacy of thinking that in following Jesus we can easily go up on the hillside and die—just like that! I admit that when Jesus was here on earth, the easiest and cheapest way to get off was to follow Jesus physically. Anyone could get out of work and say good-bye with the explanation, "I am going to follow Jesus." Multitudes did this. They followed Him physically, but they had no understanding of Him spiritually. Therefore, in that day the cheapest, easiest way to dispose of the cross was to carry it physically.

But brethren, taking our cross is not going to mean the physical act of following Jesus along a dusty pathway. We are not going to climb the hill where there are already two crosses in place and be nailed up between them.

Our cross will be determined by whatever pain and suffering and trouble which will yet come to us because of our obedience to the will of God. The true saints of God have always borne witness that wholehearted obedience brings the cross into the light quicker than anything else.

Identified with Christ

Oneness with Christ means to be identified with Christ, identified with Him in crucifixion. But we must go on to be identified with Him in resurrection as well, for beyond the cross is resurrection and the manifestation of His presence.

I would not want to make the mistake of some preachers who have never gotten beyond the message of death, death, death! They preach it so much that they never get anyone beyond death into resurrection life and victory.

I recall that when I was a young man and getting along well spiritually, having been wonderfully filled with the Holy Spirit, I read a book about the cross. In that volume, the author put you on the cross in the first chapter, and you were still hanging on the cross in the last chapter. It was gloomy all the way through—and I had a difficult time shaking that off because it was death, death, death! I was greatly helped at that time by the radiant approach of Dr. A.B. Simpson to the meaning of the cross and death to self. He took one through the meaning of the cross to the understanding that beyond the cross there is resurrection life and power, an identification with a risen Savior and the manifestation of His loving presence.

The old fifteenth-century saint* whom we have quoted declared that "God is ingenuous in making us crosses."

Considering that, we have to confess that when some Christians say, "I am crucified with Christ by faith," they are merely using a technical term and are not talking about a cross in reality. But God wants His children to know the cross. He knows that only spiritual good can come to us as a result of our identi-

---

* fifteenth-century saint: Tozer is referring to the unknown author of *The Cloud of Unknowing*.

fication with the Lord Jesus. So He is ingenuous in making crosses for us.

The quotation continues:

> He may make them of iron and of lead which are heavy of themselves. He makes some of straw which seem to weigh nothing, but one discovers that they are no less difficult to carry. A cross that appears to be of straw so that others think it amounts to nothing may be crucifying you through and through.

> He makes some with gold and precious stones which dazzle the spectators and excite the envy of the public but which crucify no less than the crosses which are more despised.

Christians who are put in high places, Christians who are entrusted with wealth and influence, know something about the kind of cross that may seem dazzling to spectators and excites the envy of the public—but if they know how to take it, it crucifies them no less than the others.

It seems that He makes our crosses of all the things we like the best so that when they turn to bitterness we are able to learn the true measure of eternal values.

It appears, also, that it often pleases God to join physical weakness to this servitude of the Spirit.

"Nothing is more useful than these two crosses together," the quote from the old saint continues. "They crucify a man from head to foot."

I confess that when I read that it came like a shock to my soul, realizing anew that Jesus Christ was crucified from head to foot! When they nailed Him there, He was crucified in every part of His body and there was no part of His holy nature that did not suffer the full intensity of those pains on the cross.

The children of God must be ready for everything the cross brings or we will surely fail the test! It is God's desire to so deal with us about all of the things that the world admires and praises that we will see them in their true light. He will treat us without pity because He desires to raise us without measure—just as He did with His own Son on the cross!

The Apostle Paul gave us this wonderful assessment of the will of God concerning the person and the earthly work of Jesus Christ: "Your attitude should be the same as that of Christ Jesus":

> Who, being in very nature God,
>   did not consider equality with God something to be grasped,
> but made himself nothing,
>   taking the very nature of a servant,
>   being made in human likeness.
> And being found in appearance as a man,
>   he humbled himself
>   and became obedient to death—even death on a cross!
>   (Philippians 2:5-8)

But notice the next word: "Therefore."

> Therefore God exalted him to the highest place
>   and gave him the name that is above every name,
> that at the name of Jesus every knee should bow . . .
> and every tongue confess!
>   (2:9-11)

This is why I believe that God will crucify without pity those whom He desires to raise without measure! This is why we believers have to surrender to Him the full control of everything that we consider to be an asset in terms of human power and talent and accomplishment. God takes pleasure in confounding everything that comes under the guise of human power—which is really weakness disguised! Our intellectual power, our great mind, our array of talents—all of these are good if God has so ordered, but in reality they are human weaknesses disguised. God wants to crucify us from head to foot—making our own powers ridiculous and useless—in the desire to raise us without measure for His glory and for our eternal good.

Dare we realize what a gracious thing it is that the Lord of all creation is desirous of raising us into a position of such glory and usefulness? Can we conceive that God would speak to angels and all the creatures who do His will and say of us: "The lid is off for this child of mine! There is to be no ceiling, no measure on what he can have, and there is no limit to where I may take him. Just keep it open. Without measure I will raise him because without pity I have been able to crucify him!"

You who are parents and you who have had the care of children know what it is to chasten without pity and yet at the same time discipline and punish with both love and pity. What do you do when you want your child to be the very finest example of manhood and character and citizenship? You pray for him and you love him so much that you would give the blood out of your veins for him—yet without pity you apply the rod of discipline and chastening. It is actually pity that makes you punish him without pity!

That sounds like a beautiful mix-up, but that is the character and desire of our God for us if we are His children. It is the love and the pity of God for His children that prescribes the chastening of a cross so that we may become the kind of mature believers and disciples that He wants us to be.

Be Completely Separated

I earnestly believe that God is trying to raise up a company of Christians in our day who are willing to be completely separated from all prejudices and all carnal desires. He wants those who are ready to put themselves at God's disposal, willing to bear any kind of cross—iron or lead or straw or gold or whatever—and to be the kinds of examples He needs on this earth.

The great question is: Is there a readiness, an eagerness among us for the kind of cross He wants to reveal through us?

Often we sing, "Hold Thou Thy cross before my closing eyes; / Shine through the gloom and point me to the skies."

What a pathetic thing to see the cross so misunderstood in sections of Christianity. Think of poor souls who have never found the evangelical meaning and assurance of atonement and justification, cleansing and pardon. When they come to the time of death, the best they know is to clutch some manufactured cross to the breast, holding it tightly and hoping for some power to come from painted metal or carved wood to take them safely over the river.

No, no! That is not the kind of cross that helps. The cross that we want is that which will come to us from being in the will of God. It is not a cross on a hill nor a cross on a church. It is not the cross that can be worn around the neck. It must be the cross of obedience to the will of God, and we must embrace it, each believer for himself!

Section V. The Radical Cross:

Its Provision

CHAPTER 19

The Need for Self-Judgment

Between deeds and consequences there is a relationship as close and inescapable as that which exists between the seed and the harvest.

We are moral beings and as such we must accept the consequence of every deed done and every word spoken. We cannot act apart from the concept of right and wrong. By our very nature we are compelled to own a three-dimensional moral obligation every time we exercise the right of choice; namely, the obligation to God, to ourselves and to others. No conscious moral being can be imagined to exist for even one moment in a nonmoral situation.

The whole question of right and wrong, of moral responsibility, of justice and judgment and reward and punishment, is sharply accented for us by the fact that we are members of a fallen race, occupying a position halfway between hell and heaven, with the knowledge of good and evil inherent within our intricate natures, along with ability to turn toward good and an inborn propensity to turn toward evil.

The present state of the human race before God is probationary. The world is on trial. The voice of God sounds over the earth, "Behold I set before you the way of life and the way of death. Choose you this day."

It has been held by most Jews and Christians that the period of probation for the individual ends with his death and after that comes the judgment. This belief is supported completely by the Scriptures of the Old and New Testaments, and any variance from this view is the result of the introduction of nonscriptural concepts into Christian thinking.

The cross of Christ has altered somewhat the position of certain persons before the judgment of God. Toward those who embrace the provisions of mercy that center around the death and resurrection of Christ one phase of judgment is no longer operative. "Whoever hears my word and believes him who sent me has eternal life and will not be condemned; he has crossed over from death to life" (John 5:24).

That is the way our Lord stated this truth, and we have only to know that the word *condemned* as it occurs here is actually "judgment" to see that for believers the consequences of sinful deeds have, in at least one aspect, been remitted.

When Christ died in the darkness for us men He made it possible for God to remit the penalty of the broken law, re-establish repentant sinners in His favor exactly as if they had never sinned and do the whole thing without relaxing the severity of the law or compromising the high demands of justice (see Romans 3:24-26).

This is a mystery too high for us and we honor God more by believing without understanding than by trying to understand. The Just died for the unjust; and because He did, the unjust may now live with the Just in complete moral congruity. Thanks be to God for His unspeakable gift.

Does this mean that the redeemed man has no responsibility to God for his conduct? Does it mean that now that he is clothed with the righteousness of Christ he will never be called to account for his deeds? God forbid! How could the moral Governor of the universe release a segment of that universe from the moral law of deeds and consequences and hope to uphold the order of the world?

Within the household of God among the redeemed and justified there is law as well as grace; not the law of Moses that knew no mercy, but the kindly law of the Father's heart that requires and expects of His children lives lived in conformity to the commandments of Christ.

If these words should startle anyone, so let it be and more also, for our Lord has told us plainly and has risen up early and sent His apostles to tell us that we must all give account of the deeds done in the body. And He has warned us faithfully of the danger that we will have for our reward only wood, hay and stubble in the day of Christ (see Romans 14:7-12; 1 Corinthians 3:9-15).

The judgment unto death and hell lies behind the Christian, but the judgment seat of Christ lies ahead. There the question will not be the law of Moses, but how we have lived within the Father's household; our record will be examined for evidence of faithfulness, self-discipline, generosity beyond the demands of the law, courage before our detractors, humility, separation from the world, cross carrying and a thousand little deeds of love that could never occur to the mere legalist or to the unregenerate soul.

"If we judged ourselves," Paul said when speaking of carnal abuses in the Corinthian church, "we would not come under judgment" (1 Corinthians 11:31). This introduces at least the possibility that we may anticipate the judgment seat of Christ and prepare ourselves against it by honest self-judgment here in this life.

This deserves a lot of prayerful consideration from us. We have the Bible before us and the Holy Spirit within us. What is to hinder us from facing the judgment seat now while we can do something about it?

CHAPTER 20

Dead in Christ

The Scriptures say that every Christian believer may consider himself to have died in Christ. Give yourselves over for a time to the study of chapters 5 through 8 in the book of Romans. You will see for yourself that this is the doctrine of the Bible: When Christ became humanity, He made it possible for us to get up into deity—not to become deity but to be united with deity.

God counts Christ's death to be my death and He counts the sacrifice Christ laid down to be mine.

I repeat: "For Christ's love compels us, because we are convinced that one died for all, and therefore all died. . . . that those who live should no longer live for themselves" (2 Corinthians 5:14-15).

No man has any right to sin again now—the voice of Jesus' blood is eloquent now, one of the most eloquent sounds in the human mind.

Wherever you find Christ's church, wherever her songs are raised, wherever the prayers of her saints rise we hear the voice of Jesus' blood pleading eloquently, and witnessing that "in the blood of Christ the sins of the world died" (see 1 John 2:2).

Oh, if men and women will only believe it!

When will we realize and confess that every sin is now a moral incongruity? As believers, we are supposed to have died with Jesus Christ our Lord. When we were joined to Him in the new birth we were joined to His death. When we were joined to His rising again, it should have been plain to us that sin is now a moral incongruity in the life of a Christian.

The sinner sins because he is out there in the world—and he has never died. He is waiting to die and he will die once and later he will die the second death.

But a Christian dies with Christ and dies in Christ and dies along with Christ, so that when he lays his body down at last the Bible says he will not see death.

God will cover the eyes of all Christians when the time comes —they never see death. The Christian stops breathing and there is a burial but he does not see death—for he already died in Christ when Christ died, and he arose with Christ when Christ arose.

That is why sin is a moral incongruity in the life and deportment of the Christian believer. It is a doctrine and theology completely unknown to those whose Christianity is like a button or flower stuck on the lapel—completely external.

I believe the gospel of Jesus Christ saved me completely—therefore He asks me for total commitment. He expects me to be a disciple totally dedicated.

Joined to Jesus Christ, how can we be other than what He is? What He does, we do. Where He leads, we go. This is genuine Christianity!

Sin is now an outrage against holy blood. To sin now is to crucify the Son of God afresh. To sin now is to belittle the blood of atonement. For a Christian to sin now is to insult the holy life laid down. I cannot believe that any Christian wants to sin.

All offenses against God will either be forgiven or avenged—we can take our choice. All offenses against God, against ourselves, against humanity, against human life—all offenses will be either forgiven or avenged. There are two voices—one pleading for vengeance, the other pleading for mercy.

What a terrible thing for men and women to get old and have no prospect, no gracious promise for the long eternity before them.

But how beautiful to come up like a ripe shock of corn and know that the Father's house is open, the doors are wide open and the Father waits to receive His children one after another!

Some years ago one of our national Christian brothers from the land of Thailand gave his testimony in my hearing. He told what it had meant in his life and for his future when the missionaries came with the good news of the gospel of Christ.

He described the godly life of one of the early missionaries and then said, "He is in the Father's house now."

He told of one of the missionary women and the love of Christ she had displayed and then said, "She is in the Father's house now."

What a vision for a humble Christian who only a generation before had been a pagan, worshiping idols and spirits—and now because of grace and mercy he talks about the Father's house as though it were just a step away, across the street.

This is the gospel of Christ—the kind of Christianity I believe in. What joy to discover that God is not mad at us and that we are His children—because Jesus died for us, because the blood of Jesus "speaks a better word than the blood of Abel" (Hebrews 12:24). What a blessing to find out that the mercy of God speaks louder than the voice of justice. What a hope that makes it possible for the Lord's people to lie down quietly when the time comes and whisper, "Father, I am coming home!"

Oh, we ought to make more of the blood of the Lamb, because it is by the blood that we are saved; by the blood atonement is made.

You know I encourage you to sing some of the old camp meeting songs with plain theology and clear message. This is one of those:

> The cross, the cross, the bloodstained cross,
>   The hallowed cross I see;
> Reminding me of precious blood
>   That once was shed for me.

A thousand, thousand fountains spring
   Up from the throne of God;
But none to me such blessings bring
   As Jesus' precious blood.

That priceless blood my ransom paid
   When I in bondage stood;
On Jesus all my sins were laid,
   He saved me with His blood.

By faith that blood now sweeps away
   My sins, as like a flood;
Nor lets one guilty blemish stay;
   All praise to Jesus' blood!

This wondrous theme will best employ
   My heart before my God;
And make all heaven resound with joy
   For Jesus' cleansing blood.

The blood of Jesus Christ continues to plead eloquently. At the right hand of God the Father I do not believe that Jesus, our great high priest, has to talk and talk. I am sure His intercession for us lies in His two wounded hands.

When children of God violate the covenant, God hears the voice of the wounded Son of God and forgives, but is that reason for us to be careless? Never! Never while the world stands!

We Christians ought to be the cleanest, purest, most righteous, holiest people in all the world—for the blood of Jesus Christ can sweep away our sins "as like a flood; nor lets one guilty blemish stay; all praise to Jesus' blood!"

CHAPTER 21

Who Put Jesus on the Cross?

He was pierced for our transgressions,
he was crushed for our iniquities;
the punishment that brought us peace was upon him,
and by his wounds we are healed.
    (Isaiah 53:5)

There is a strange conspiracy of silence in the world to-day—even in religious circles—about man's responsibility for sin, the reality of judgment and about an outraged God and the necessity for a crucified Savior.

On the other hand, there is an open and powerful movement swirling throughout the world designed to give people peace of mind in relieving them of any historical responsibility for the trial and crucifixion of Jesus Christ. The problem with modern decrees and pronouncements in the name of brotherhood and tolerance is their basic misconception of Christian theology.

A great shadow lies upon every man and every woman—the fact that our Lord was bruised and wounded and crucified for the entire human race. This is the basic human responsibility that men are trying to push off and evade.

Let us not eloquently blame Judas nor Pilate. Let us not curl our lips at Judas and accuse, "He sold Him for money!"

Let us pity Pilate, the weak-willed, because he did not have courage enough to stand for the innocence of the Man whom he declared had done no wrong.

Let us not curse the Jews for delivering Jesus to be crucified. Let us not single out the Romans in blaming them for putting Jesus on the cross.

Oh, they were guilty, certainly! But they were our accomplices in crime. They and we put Him on the cross, not they alone. That rising malice and anger that burns so hotly in your being today put Him there. That basic dishonesty that comes to light in your being when you knowingly cheat and chisel on your income tax return—that put Him on the cross. The evil, the hatred, the suspicion, the jealousy, the lying tongue, the carnality, the fleshly love of pleasure—all of these in natural man joined in putting Him on the cross.

We Put Him There

We may as well admit it. Every one of us in Adam's race had a share in putting Him on the cross!

I have often wondered how any professing Christian man or woman could approach the Communion table and participate in the memorial of our Lord's death without feeling and sensing the pain and the shame of the inward confession: "I, too, am among those who helped put Him on the cross!"

I remind you that it is characteristic of the natural man to keep himself so busy with unimportant trifles that he is able to avoid the settling of the most important matters relating to life and existence.

Men and women will gather anywhere and everywhere to talk about and discuss every subject from the latest fashions on up to Plato and philosophy—up and down the scale. They talk about the necessity for peace. They may talk about the Church and how it can be a bulwark against communism. None of these things are embarrassing subjects.

But the conversation all stops and the taboo of silence becomes effective when anyone dares to suggest that there are spiritual subjects of vital importance to our souls that ought to be discussed and considered. There seems to be an unwritten rule in polite society that if any religious subjects are to be discussed, it must be within the framework of theory—"Never let it get personal!"

All the while, there is really only one thing that is of vital and lasting importance—the fact that our Lord Jesus Christ "was pierced for our transgressions, he was crushed for our iniquities; the punishment that brought us peace was upon him, and by his wounds we are healed."

There are two very strong and terrible words here—*transgressions* and *iniquities*.

A *transgression* is a breaking away, a revolt from just authority. In all of the moral universe, only man and the fallen angels have rebelled and violated the authority of God, and men are still in flagrant rebellion against that authority.

There is no expression in the English language which can convey the full weight and force of terror inherent in the words *transgression* and *iniquity*. But in man's fall and transgression against the created order and authority of God we recognize perversion and twistedness and deformity and crookedness and rebellion. These are all there, and, undeniably, they reflect the reason and the necessity for the death of Jesus Christ on the cross.

The word *iniquity* is not a good word—and God knows how we hate it! But the consequences of iniquity cannot be escaped.

The prophet reminds us clearly that the Savior was crushed for "our iniquities."

We deny it and say, "No!" But the fingerprints of all mankind are plain evidence against us. The authorities have no trouble finding and apprehending the awkward burglar who leaves his fingerprints on tables and doorknobs, for they have his record. So, the fingerprints of man are found in every dark cellar and in every alley and in every dimly lighted evil place throughout the world—every man's fingerprints are recorded and God knows man from man. It is impossible to escape our guilt and place our moral responsibilities upon someone else. It is a highly personal matter—"our iniquities."

The Breadth of His Wounding

For our iniquities and our transgressions He was bruised and wounded. I do not even like to tell you of the implications of His wounding. It really means that He was profaned and broken, stained and defiled. He was Jesus Christ when men took Him into their evil hands. Soon He was humiliated and profaned. They plucked out His beard. He was stained with His own blood, defiled with earth's grime. Yet He accused no one and He cursed no one. He was Jesus Christ, the wounded One.

Israel's great burden and amazing blunder was her judgment that this wounded One on the hillside beyond Jerusalem was being punished for His own sin.

Isaiah foresaw this historic error in judgment, and he himself was a Jew, saying: "We thought He was smitten of God. We thought that God was punishing Him for His own iniquity for we did not know then that God was punishing Him for our transgressions and our iniquities."

He was profaned for our sakes. He who is the second Person of the Godhead was not only wounded for us, but He was profaned by ignorant and unworthy men.

Isaiah reported that "the punishment that brought us peace was upon him."

How few there are who realize that it is this peace—the health and prosperity and welfare and safety of the individual—which restores us to God. A chastisement fell upon Him so that we as individual humans could experience peace with God if we so desired. But the chastisement was upon Him. Rebuke, discipline and correction—these are found in chastisement. He was beaten and scourged in public by the decree of the Romans. They lashed Him in public view as they later lashed Paul. They whipped and punished Him in full view of the jeering public, and His bruised and bleeding and swollen person was the answer to the peace of the world and to the peace of the human heart. He was chastised for our peace; the blows fell upon Him.

I do not suppose there is any more humiliating punishment ever devised by mankind than that of whipping and flogging grown men in public view. Many men who have been put in a jail have become a kind of hero in the eye of the public. Heavy fines have been assessed against various offenders of the law, but it is not unusual for such an offender to boast and brag about his escape. But when a bad man is taken out before a laughing, jeering crowd, stripped to the waist and soundly whipped like a child—a bad child—he loses face and has no boasting left. He will probably never be the bold, bad man he was before. That kind of whipping and chastisement breaks the spirit and humiliates. The chagrin is worse than the lash that falls on the back.

I speak for myself as a forgiven and justified sinner, and I think I speak for a great host of forgiven and born-again men and women, when I say that in our repentance we sensed just a fraction and just a token of the wounding and chastisement which fell upon Jesus Christ as He stood in our place and in our behalf. A truly penitent man who has realized the enormity of his sin and rebellion against God senses a violent revulsion against himself—he does not feel that he can actually dare to ask God to let him off. But peace has been established, for the blows have fallen on Jesus Christ. He was publicly humiliated and disgraced as a common thief, wounded and bruised and bleeding under the lash for sins He did not commit, for rebellions in which He had no part, for iniquity in the human stream that was an outrage to a loving God and Creator.

The Significance of His Stripes

Isaiah sums up his message of a substitutionary atonement with the good news that "by his wounds we are healed."

The meaning of these "wounds" in the original language is not a pleasant description. It means to be actually hurt and injured until the entire body is black and blue as one great bruise.

Mankind has always used this kind of bodily laceration as a punitive measure. Society has always insisted upon the right to punish a man for his own wrongdoing. The punishment is generally suited to the nature of the crime. It is a kind of revenge—society taking vengeance against the person who dared flout the rules.

But the suffering of Jesus Christ was not punitive. It was not for Himself and not for punishment of anything that He Himself had done.

The suffering of Jesus was corrective. He was willing to suffer in order that He might correct us and perfect us, so that His suffering might not begin and end in suffering, but that it might begin in suffering and end in healing.

Brethren, that is the glory of the cross! That is the glory of the kind of sacrifice that was for so long in the heart of God! That is the glory of the kind of atonement that allows a repentant sinner to come into peaceful and gracious fellowship with his God and Creator! It began in His suffering and it ended in our healing. It began in His wounds and ended in our purification. It began in His bruises and ended in our cleansing.

What is our repentance? I discover that repentance is mainly remorse for the share we had in the revolt that wounded Jesus Christ, our Lord. Further, I have discovered that truly repentant men never quite get over it, for repentance is not a state of mind and spirit that takes its leave as soon as God has given forgiveness and as soon as cleansing is realized.

That painful and acute conviction that accompanies repentance may well subside and a sense of peace and cleansing come, but even the holiest of justified men will think back over his part in the wounding and the chastisement of the Lamb of God. A sense of shock will still come over him. A sense of wonder will remain—wonder that the Lamb that was wounded should turn His wounds into the cleansing and forgiveness of one who wounded Him.

This brings to mind a gracious moving in many of our evangelical church circles—a willingness to move toward the spiritual purity of heart taught and exemplified so well by John Wesley in a time of spiritual dryness.

In spite of the fact that the word *sanctification* is a good Bible word, we have experienced a period in which evangelical churches hardly dared breathe the word because of the fear of being classified among the "holy rollers."

Not only is the good word *sanctification* coming back, but I am hopeful that what the word stands for in the heart and mind of God is coming back too. The believing Christian, the child of God, should have a holy longing and desire for the pure heart and clean hands that are a delight to his Lord. It was for this that Jesus Christ allowed Himself to be humiliated, maltreated, lacerated. He was bruised, wounded and chastised so that the people of God could be a cleansed and spiritual people—in order that our minds might be pure and our thoughts pure. This provision all began in His suffering and ends in our cleansing. It began with His open, bleeding wounds and ends in peaceful hearts and calm and joyful demeanor in His people.

Amazement at the Mystery of Godliness

Every humble and devoted believer in Jesus Christ must have his own periods of wonder and amazement at this mystery of godliness—the willingness of the Son of Man to take our place in judgment and in punishment. If the amazement has all gone out of it, something is wrong, and you need to have the stony ground broken up again!

I often remind you that Paul, one of the holiest men who ever lived, was not ashamed of his times of remembrance and wonder over the grace and kindness of God. He knew that God did not hold his old sins against him forever. Knowing the account was all settled, Paul's happy heart assured him again and again that all was well. At the same time, Paul could only shake his head in amazement and confess: "I am unworthy to be called, but by His grace, I am a new creation in Jesus Christ!" (see 2 Corinthians 5:17).

I make this point about the faith and assurance and rejoicing of Paul in order to say that if that humble sense of perpetual penance ever leaves our justified being, we are on the way to backsliding.

Charles Finney, one of the greatest of all of God's men throughout the years, testified that in the midst of his labors and endeavors in bringing men to Christ, he would at times sense a coldness in his own heart.

Finney did not excuse it. In his writings he told of having to turn from all of his activities, seeking God's face and Spirit anew in fasting and prayer.

"I plowed up until I struck fire and met God," he wrote. What a helpful and blessed formula for the concerned children of God in every generation!

Those who compose the Body of Christ, His Church, must be inwardly aware of two basic facts if we are to be joyfully effective for our Lord.

We must have the positive knowledge that we are clean through His wounds, with God's peace realized through His stripes. This is how God assures us that we may be all right inside. In this spiritual condition, we will treasure the purity of His cleansing and we will not excuse any evil or wrongdoing.

Also, we must keep upon us a joyful and compelling sense of gratitude for the bruised and wounded One, our Lord Jesus Christ. Oh, what a mystery of redemption—that the bruises of One healed the bruises of many; that the wounds of One healed the wounds of millions; that the stripes of One healed the stripes of many.

The wounds and bruises that should have fallen upon us fell upon Him, and we are saved for His sake!

Many years ago, a historic group of Presbyterians were awed by the wonder and the mystery of Christ's having come in the flesh to give Himself as an offering for every man's sin.

Those humble Christians said to one another: "Let us walk softly and search our hearts and wait on God and seek His face throughout the next three months. Then we will come to the

Communion table with our hearts prepared—lest the table of our Lord should become a common and careless thing."

God still seeks humble, cleansed and trusting hearts through which to reveal His divine power and grace and life. A professional botanist from the university can describe the acacia bush of the desert better than Moses could ever do—but God is still looking for the humble souls who are not satisfied until God speaks with the divine fire in the bush.

A research scientist could be employed to stand and tell us more about the elements and properties found in bread and wine than the apostles ever knew. But this is our danger: We may have lost the light and warmth of the presence of God, and we may have only bread and wine. The fire will have gone from the bush, and the glory will not be in our act of Communion and fellowship.

It is not so important that we know all of the history and all of the scientific facts, but it is vastly important that we desire and know and cherish the presence of the living God, who has given "Jesus Christ, the Righteous One. He is the atoning sacrifice for our sins, and not only for ours but also for the sins of the whole world" (1 John 2:1-2).

Section VI. The Radical Cross:
Its Paradox

CHAPTER 22

We Must Die
If We Would Live

Let me die—lest I die—only let me see Thy face." That was the prayer of St. Augustine.

"Hide not Thy face from me," he cried in an agony of desire. "Oh! That I might repose on Thee. Oh! That Thou wouldst enter into my heart, and inebriate it, that I may not forget my ills, and embrace Thee, my sole good."

This longing to die, to get our opaque form out of the way so that it might not hide from us the lovely face of God, is one that is instantly understood by the hungry-hearted believer. To die that we might not die! There is no contradiction here, for there are before us two kinds of dying, a dying to be sought and a dying to be avoided at any cost.

To Augustine the sight of God inwardly enjoyed was life itself and anything less than that was death. To exist in total eclipse under the shadow of nature without the realized Presence was a condition not to be tolerated. Whatever hid God's face from him must be taken out of the way, even his own self-love, his dearest ego, his most cherished treasures. So he prayed, "Let me die."

The great saint's daring prayer was heard and, as might be expected, was answered with a fullness of generosity characteristic of God. He died the kind of death to which Paul testified: "I have been crucified with Christ and I no longer live, but

Christ lives in me" (Galatians 2:20). His life and ministry continued and his presence is always there, in his books, in the Church, in history; but wondrous as it may be, he is strangely transparent; his own personality is scarcely seen, while the light of Christ shines through with a kind of healing splendor.

There have been those who have thought that to get themselves out of the way it was necessary to withdraw from society; so they denied all natural human relationships and went into the desert or the mountain or the hermit's cell to fast and labor and struggle to mortify their flesh. While their motive was good it is impossible to commend their method. It is altogether too tough to be killed by abusing the body or starving the affections. It yields to nothing less than the cross.

In every Christian's heart there is a cross and a throne, and the Christian is on the throne till he puts himself on the cross; if he refuses the cross he remains on the throne. Perhaps this is at the bottom of the backsliding and worldliness among gospel believers today. We want to be saved but we insist that Christ do all the dying. No cross for us, no dethronement, no dying. We remain king within the little kingdom of Mansoul and wear our tinsel crown with all the pride of a Caesar; but we doom ourselves to shadows and weakness and spiritual sterility.

If we will not die then we must die, and that death will mean the forfeiture of many of those everlasting treasures which the saints have cherished. Our uncrucified flesh will rob us of purity of heart, Christlikeness of character, spiritual insight, fruitfulness; and more than all, it will hide from us the vision of God's face, that vision which has been the light of earth and will be the completeness of heaven.

CHAPTER 23

That Incredible Christian

The current effort of so many religious leaders to harmonize Christianity with science, philosophy and every natural and reasonable thing is, I believe, the result of failure to understand Christianity and, judging from what I have heard and read, failure to understand science and philosophy as well.

At the heart of the Christian system lies the cross of Christ with its divine paradox. The power of Christianity appears in its antipathy toward, never in its agreement with, the ways of fallen men. The truth of the cross is revealed in its contradictions. The witness of the Church is most effective when she declares rather than explains, for the gospel is addressed not to reason but to faith. What can be proved requires no faith to accept. Faith rests upon the character of God, not upon the demonstrations of laboratory or logic.

The cross stands in bold opposition to the natural man. Its philosophy runs contrary to the processes of the unregenerate mind, so that Paul could say bluntly that the preaching of the cross is to them that perish foolishness. To try to find a common ground between the message of the cross and man's fallen reason is to try the impossible, and if persisted in must result in an impaired reason, a meaningless cross and a powerless Christianity.

But let us bring the whole matter down from the uplands of theory and simply observe the true Christian as he puts into

practice the teachings of Christ and His apostles. Note the contradictions:

The Christian believes that in Christ he has died, yet he is
more alive than before and he fully expects to live forever. He
walks on earth while seated in heaven and though born on
earth he finds that after his conversion he is not at home here.
Like the nighthawk, which in the air is the essence of grace and
beauty but on the ground is awkward and ugly, so the Christian appears at his best in the heavenly places but does not fit
well into the ways of the very society into which he was born.

The Christian soon learns that if he would be victorious as a
son of heaven among men on earth he must not follow the
common pattern of mankind, but rather the contrary. That he
may be safe he puts himself in jeopardy; he loses his life to save
it and is in danger of losing it if he attempts to preserve it. He
goes down to get up. If he refuses to go down he is already
down, but when he starts down he is on his way up.

He is strongest when he is weakest and weakest when he is
strong. Though poor he has the power to make others rich, but
when he becomes rich his ability to enrich others vanishes. He
has most after he has given most away and has least when he
possesses most.

He may be and often is highest when he feels lowest and
most sinless when he is most conscious of sin. He is wisest
when he knows that he knows not and knows least when he
has acquired the greatest amount of knowledge. He sometimes
does most by doing nothing and goes furthest when standing
still. In heaviness he manages to rejoice and keeps his heart
glad even in sorrow.

The paradoxical character of the Christian is revealed constantly. For instance, he believes that he is saved now, nevertheless he expects to be saved later and looks forward joyfully
to future salvation. He fears God but is not afraid of Him. In
God's presence he feels overwhelmed and undone, yet there is
nowhere he would rather be than in that presence. He knows

that he has been cleansed from his sin, yet he is painfully conscious that in his flesh dwells no good thing.

He loves supremely One whom he has never seen, and though himself poor and lowly he talks familiarly with One who is King of all kings and Lord of all lords, and is aware of no incongruity in so doing. He feels that he is in his own right altogether less than nothing, yet he believes without question that he is the apple of God's eye and that for him the Eternal Son became flesh and died on the cross of shame.

The Christian is a citizen of heaven and to that sacred citizenship he acknowledges first allegiance; yet he may love his earthly country with that intensity of devotion that caused John Knox to pray, "O God, give me Scotland or I die."

He cheerfully expects before long to enter that bright world above, but he is in no hurry to leave this world and is quite willing to await the summons of his heavenly Father. And he is unable to understand why the critical unbeliever should condemn him for this; it all seems so natural and right in the circumstances that he sees nothing inconsistent about it.

The cross-carrying Christian, furthermore, is both a confirmed pessimist and an optimist the like of which is to be found nowhere else on earth.

When he looks at the cross he is a pessimist, for he knows that the same judgment that fell on the Lord of glory condemns in that one act all nature and all the world of men. He rejects every human hope out of Christ because he knows that man's noblest effort is only dust building on dust.

Yet he is calmly, restfully optimistic. If the cross condemns the world the resurrection of Christ guarantees the ultimate triumph of good throughout the universe. Through Christ all will be well at last and the Christian waits the consummation. Incredible Christian!

CHAPTER 24

Integration or Repudiation?

The world seems to possess a real genius for being wrong, even the educated world. We might just let that pass and go fishing except that we Christians happen to be living in the world and we have an obligation to be right—in everything, all of the time. We cannot afford to be wrong.

I can see how a right man might live in a wrong world and not be much affected by it except that the world will not let him alone. It wants to educate him. It is forever coming up with some new idea, which, by the way, is usually an old idea dusted off and shined up for the occasion and demanding that everyone, including the said right man, conform on pain of deep-seated frustration or a horrible complex of some kind.

Society, being fluid, usually moves like the wind, going all out in one direction until the novelty wears off or there is a war or a depression. Then the breeze sets another way and everyone is supposed to go along with it without asking too many questions, though this constant change of direction should certainly cause the thoughtful soul to wonder whether anyone really knows what all the excitement is about after all.

Right now the zephyrs are blowing in the direction of social integration, sometimes also called social adjustment. According to this notion society is possessed of a norm, a sort of best-of-all-possible model after which we must all pattern ourselves if we want to escape sundry psychosomatic disorders and emotional upsets. The only safety for any of us is in becoming so well adjusted to the other members of society as to reduce the nervous and mental friction to a minimum. Education therefore should first of all teach adjustment to society. Whatever people happen to be interested in at the moment must be accepted as normal, and any nonconformity on the part of anyone is bad for the individual and harmful to everybody. Our highest ambition should be to become integrated to the mass, to lose our moral individuality in the whole.

However absurd this may appear when thus stated baldly it is nevertheless a fair description of the most popular brand of philosophy now engaging the attention of society. So many and so efficient are the media of mass communication that when the Brahmans* of the educational world decide that it is time for the wind to change, the common people quickly get the drift and swing obediently into the breeze. Anyone who resists is a killjoy and a spoilsport, to say nothing of being old-fashioned and dogmatic.

Well, if to escape the charge of being dogmatic I must accept the changing dogmas of the masses, then I am willing to be known as a dogmatist and no holds barred. We who call ourselves Christians are supposed to be a people apart. We claim to have repudiated the wisdom of this world and adopted the wisdom of the cross as the guide of our lives. We have thrown in our lot with that One who while He lived on earth was the most unadjusted of the sons of men. He would not be integrated into society. He stood above it and condemned it by withdrawing from it even while dying for it. Die for it He would, but surrender to it He would not.

The wisdom of the cross is repudiation of the world's "norm." Christ, not society, becomes the pattern of the Christian life. The believer seeks adjustment, not to the world, but to

---

* Brahman: literally, this word refers to a Hindu of the highest social caste in India. Tozer uses the word to mean a person of high social standing and cultivated intellect.

the will of God, and just to the degree that he is integrated into the heart of Christ is he out of adjustment with fallen human society. The Christian sees the world as a sinking ship from which he escapes not by integration but by abandonment.

A new moral power will flow back into the Church when we stop preaching social adjustment and begin to preach social repudiation and cross carrying. Modern Christians hope to save the world by being like it, but it will never work. The Church's power over the world springs out of her unlikeness to it, never from her integration into it.

CHAPTER 25

Protected by
the Blood of Christ

We have been told in Congress that the lives of forty million Americans could be saved if we as Americans take precautions to shield ourselves from the fallout if a hydrogen bomb should fall on our country.

I don't know whether the angel of death will spread his wings on the blast known as an H-bomb or not, but I know that our sins have brought the anger of God against us, and I know that all over the civilized world there is the shadow of the oncoming angel of death.

I have absolutely no hope that there is any way to escape, except we believe God and take the blood and put it upon the doorposts and lintels and there abide, believing simply that God cannot break His word and that He who has spoken will also perform.

The blood that I refer to, of course, is the blood shed once on the cross of Christ.

Here God's Lamb was slain. It was Abraham's lamb, Abel's lamb, Isaiah's lamb, and Levi's and Moses' lamb. Theirs was provisional for the time, but when God's Lamb was slain, no other dared be slain after that.

As long as God's Lamb had not been selected for the world to examine and had not been slain, they could slay other lambs. It would be their lamb, the lamb that belonged to this or that house, and there were hundreds of thousands of them slain during the long course of Israel's history.

But when God set His Lamb before the world, and the world examined Him critically for thirty-three years and found Him without fault, and God slew that Lamb and offered Him as a sacrifice, no other lamb dared be offered!

Now, that's the blood I recommend. They got the blood on the doorpost by sprinkling it. They took a sponge-like plant called hyssop and dipped it in the blood and sprinkled it on the doorposts.

The hyssop was a common plant, growing everyplace.

So, you and I have faith, and by faith we protect ourselves. I would not—dare not—go out under the angry sky until I have known and do know that the blood of Jesus Christ is upon the lintel and door of my heart!

"This is how you are to eat it: with your cloak tucked into your belt, your sandals on your feet and your staff in your hand. Eat it in haste; it is the LORD'S Passover" (Exodus 12:11).

Christians are never to be caught unawares. They are never to put on their smoking jacket or the lounging robe while it is dark and the call of the trumpet is expected. The only safety for anyone is the blood. While the call of God may come at any minute to take us out of this Egypt we call the world, you and I cannot afford to be careless.

Instead of letting the cross keep us always on the alert and ready to go, we have painted the cross and reshaped it and geared it in with the better element of the world. The people of God are asleep doing their little labors while we wait for the call of the trumpet that will take us out of this world.

Oh, that we might again have that sense of immediacy and urgency that was upon the early Church!

CHAPTER 26

Take Up Your Cross

"If any *man* will come after me, let him deny himself, and take up his cross, and follow me" (Matthew 16:24, KJV).

It is like the Lord to fasten a world upon nothing, and make it stay in place. Here He takes that wonderful, mysterious microcosm we call the human soul and makes its future well-being or suffering to rest upon a single word—*if*. "If any man," He says, and teaches at once the universal inclusiveness of His invitation and the freedom of the human will. Everyone may come; no one need come, and whoever does come, comes because he chooses to.

Every man holds his future in his hand. Not the dominant world leader only, but the inarticulate man lost in anonymity is a "man of destiny." He decides which way his soul shall go. He chooses, and destiny waits on the nod of his head. He decides, and hell enlarges herself, or heaven prepares another mansion. So much of Himself has God given to men.

There is a strange beauty in the ways of God with men. He sends salvation to the world in the person of a Man and sends that Man to walk the busy ways saying, "If any man will come after me." No drama, no fanfare, no tramp of marching feet or tumult of shouting. A kindly Stranger walks through the earth, and so quiet is His voice that it is sometimes lost in the hurly-burly; but it is the last voice of God, and until we become quiet to hear it we have no authentic message. He bears good tidings from afar but He compels no man to listen. "If any man will," He says, and passes on. Friendly, courteous, unobtrusive, He yet bears the signet of the King. His word is divine authority, His eyes a tribunal, His face a last judgment.

"If any man will come after me," He says, and some will rise and go after Him, but others give no heed to His voice. So the gulf opens between man and man, between those who will and those who will not. Silently, terribly the work goes on, as each one decides whether he will hear or ignore the voice of invitation. Unknown to the world, perhaps unknown even to the individual, the work of separation takes place. Each hearer of the Voice must decide for himself, and he must decide on the basis of the evidence the message affords. There will be no thunder sound, no heavenly sign or light from heaven. The Man is His own proof. The marks in His hands and feet are the insignia of His rank and office. He will not put Himself again on trial; He will not argue, but the morning of the judgment will confirm what men in the twilight have decided.

And those who would follow Him must accept His conditions. "Let him," He says, and there is no appeal from His words. He will use no coercion, but neither will He compromise. Men cannot make the terms; they merely agree to them. Thousands turn from Him because they will not meet His conditions. He watches them as they go, for He loves them, but He will make no concessions. Admit one soul into the kingdom by compromise and that kingdom is no longer secure. Christ will be Lord, or He will be Judge. Every man must decide whether he will take Him as Lord now or face Him as Judge then.

What are the terms of discipleship? Only one with a perfect knowledge of mankind could have dared to make them. Only the Lord of men could have risked the effect of such rigorous demands: "Let him deny himself." We hear these words and shake our heads in astonishment. Can we have heard aright? Can the Lord lay down such severe rules at the door of the kingdom? He can and He does. If He is to save the man, He must save him from himself. It is the "himself" which has en-

slaved and corrupted the man. Deliverance comes only by denial of that self. No man in his own strength can shed the
chains with which self has bound him, but in the next breath
the Lord reveals the source of the power which is to set the
soul free: "Let him . . . take up his cross." The cross has gathered in the course of the years much of beauty and symbolism,
but the cross of which Jesus spoke had nothing of beauty in it.
It was an instrument of death. Slaying men was its only func-
tion. Men did not wear that cross; but that cross wore men. It
stood naked until a man was pinned on it, a living man fas-
tened like some grotesque stickpin on its breast to writhe and
groan till death stilled and silenced him. That is the cross.
Nothing less. And when it is robbed of its tears and blood and
pain it is the cross no longer. "Let him . . . take up *his* [empha-
sis added] cross," said Jesus, and in death he will know deliverance from himself.

A strange thing under the sun is crossless Christianity. The
cross of Christendom is a no-cross, an ecclesiastical symbol.
The cross of Christ is a place of death. Let each one be careful
which cross he carries.

"And follow me." Now the glory begins to break in upon the
soul that has just returned from Calvary. "Follow me" is an invitation and a challenge and a promise. The cross has been the
end of a life and the beginning of a life. The life that ended
there was a life of sin and slavery; the life that began there is a
life of holiness and spiritual freedom. "And follow me," He
says, and faith runs on tiptoe to keep pace with the advancing
light. Until we know the program of our risen Lord for all the
years to come we can never know everything He meant when
He invited us to follow Him. Each heart can have its own
dream of fair worlds and new revelations, of the odyssey of the
ransomed soul in the ages to come, but whoever follows Jesus
will find at last that He has made the reality to outrun the
dream.

Section VII. The Radical Cross:
Its Promise

CHAPTER 27

What Easter Is About

The celebration of Easter began very early in the Church and has continued without interruption to this day. There is scarcely a church anywhere but will observe the day in some manner, whether it be by simply singing a resurrection hymn or by the performance of the most elaborate rites.

Ignoring the etymological derivation of the word *Easter* and the controversy that once gathered around the question of the date on which it should be observed, and admitting as we must that to millions the whole thing is little more than a pagan festival, I want to ask and try to answer two questions about Easter.

The first question is, What is Easter all about? and the second, What practical meaning does it have for the plain Christian of today?

The first may be answered briefly or its answer could run into a thousand pages. The real significance of the day stems from an event, a solid historical incident that took place on a certain day in a geographical location that can be identified on any good map of the world. It was first announced by the two men who stood beside the empty tomb and said simply, "He is not here; he has risen" (Matthew 28:6), and was later affirmed in the solemnly beautiful words of one who saw Him after His resurrection:

But Christ has indeed been raised from the dead, the firstfruits of those who have fallen asleep. For since death came through a man, the resurrection of the dead comes also through a man. For as in Adam all die, so in Christ all will be made alive. But each in his own turn: Christ, the firstfruits; then, when he comes, those who belong to him. (1 Corinthians 15:20–23)

That is what Easter is about. The Man called Jesus is alive after having been publicly put to death by crucifixion. The Roman soldiers nailed Him to the cross and watched Him till the life had gone from Him. Then a responsible company of persons, headed by one Joseph of Arimathea, took the body down from the cross and laid it in a tomb, after which the Roman authorities sealed the tomb and set a watch before it to make sure the body would not be stolen away by zealous but misguided disciples. This last precaution was the brain child of the priests and the Pharisees, and how it backfired on them is known to the ages, for it went far to confirm the fact that the body was completely dead and that it could have gotten out of the tomb only by some miracle.

In spite of the tomb and the watch and the seal, in spite of death itself, the Man who had been laid in the place of death walked out alive after three days. That is the simple historical fact attested by more than 500 trustworthy persons, among them being a man who is said by some scholars to have had one of the mightiest intellects of all time. That man of course was Saul, who later became a disciple of Jesus and was known as Paul the apostle. This is what the Church has believed and celebrated throughout the centuries. This is what the Church celebrates today.

Granted that this is all true, what does it or can it mean to us who live so far removed in space from the event and so far away in time? Several thousand miles and nearly two thousand years separate us from that first bright Easter morning. Apart from or in addition to the joy of returning spring and the sweet music and the sense of cheerfulness associated with the day, what practical significance does Easter have for us?

To borrow the words of Paul, "Much in every way!" (Romans 3:2). For one thing, any question about Christ's death was forever cleared away by His resurrection. He "through the Spirit of holiness was declared with power to be the Son of God by his resurrection from the dead" (1:4). Also His place in the intricate web of Old Testament prophecy was fully established when He arose. When He walked with the two discouraged disciples after His resurrection, He chided them for their unbelief and then asked, "'Did not the Christ have to suffer these things and then enter his glory?' And beginning with Moses and all the Prophets, he explained to them what was said in all the Scriptures concerning himself" (Luke 24:26–27).

Then it should be remembered that He could not save us by the cross alone. He must rise from the dead to give validity to His finished work. A dead Christ would be as helpless as the ones He tried to save. He "was raised to life for our justification" (Romans 4:25), said Paul, and in so saying declared that our hope of righteousness depended upon our Lord's ability to beat death and rise beyond its power.

It is of great practical importance to us to know that *the Christ who lived again still lives.* "Therefore let all Israel be assured of this: God has made this Jesus, whom you crucified, both Lord and Christ" (Acts 2:36), said Peter on the day of Pentecost; and this accorded with our Lord's own words, "All authority in heaven and on earth has been given to me" (Matthew 28:18), and with the words of Hebrews, "The point of what we are saying is this: We do have such a high priest, who sat down at the right hand of the throne of the Majesty in heaven" (8:1).

Not only does He still live, but *He can never die again.* "For we know that since Christ was raised from the dead, he cannot die again; death no longer has mastery over him" (Romans 6:9).

Finally, all that Christ is, all that He has accomplished for us is available to us now if we obey and trust.

We are more than conquerors, through our Captain's triumph;
    Let us shout the victory as we onward go.

CHAPTER 28

The Cross Did Not Change God

The cross did not change God. "I the LORD do not change" (Malachi 3:6).

The work of Christ on the cross did not influence God to love us, did not increase that love by one degree, did not open any fount of grace or mercy in His heart. He had loved us from old eternity and needed nothing to stimulate that love. The cross is not responsible for God's love; rather it was His love which conceived the cross as the one method by which we could be saved.

God felt no different toward us after Christ had died for us, for in the mind of God Christ had already died before the foundation of the world. God never saw us except through atonement. The human race could not have existed one day in its fallen state had not Christ spread His mantle of atonement over it. And this He did in eternal purpose long ages before they led Him out to die on the hill above Jerusalem. All God's dealings with man have been conditioned upon the cross.

Much unworthy thinking has been done about the cross, and a lot of injurious teaching has resulted. The idea that Christ rushed in breathless to catch the upraised arm of God ready to descend in fury upon us is not drawn from the Bible. It has arisen from the necessary limitations of human speech in attempting to set forth the fathomless mystery of atonement.

Neither is the picture of Christ going out trembling to the cross to appease the wrath of God in accordance with the truth. The Scriptures never represent the Persons of the Trinity as opposed to or in disagreement with each other. The Holy Three have ever been and will forever be one in essence, in love, in purpose.

We have been redeemed not by one Person of the Trinity putting Himself against another but by the three Persons working in the ancient and glorious harmony of the Godhead.

CHAPTER 29

Grace: The Only Means of Salvation

Here are two important truths. (And I want you to take it and the next time you hear a professor or a preacher say otherwise, go to him and remind him of this.) The first truth is that no one ever was saved, no one is now saved and no one ever will be saved except by grace. Before Moses nobody was ever saved except by grace. During Moses' time nobody was ever saved except by grace. After Moses and before the cross and after the cross and since the cross and during all that dispensation, during any dispensation, anywhere, any time since Abel offered his first lamb before God on the smoking altar—nobody was ever saved in any other way than by grace.

The second truth is that grace always comes by Jesus Christ. The law was given by Moses, but grace came by Jesus Christ. This does not mean that before Jesus was born of Mary there was no grace. God dealt in grace with mankind, looking forward to the Incarnation and death of Jesus before Christ came. Now, since He's come and gone to the Father's right hand, God looks back upon the cross as we look back upon the cross. Everybody from Abel on was saved by looking forward to the cross. Grace came by Jesus Christ. And everybody that's been saved since the cross is saved by looking back at the cross.

Grace always comes by Jesus Christ. It didn't come at His birth, but it came in God's ancient plan. No grace was ever administered to anybody except by and through and in Jesus Christ. When Adam and Eve had no children, God spared Adam and Eve by grace. And when they had their two boys, one offered a lamb and thus said, "I look forward to the Lamb of God." He accepted the grace of Christ Jesus thousands of years before He was born, and God gave him witness that he was justified.

The grace did not come when Christ was born in a manger. It did not come when Christ was baptized or anointed of the Spirit. It did not come when He died on a cross; it did not come when He rose from the dead. It did not come when He went to the Father's right hand. Grace came from the ancient beginnings through Jesus Christ the eternal Son and was manifest on the cross of Calvary, in fiery blood and tears and sweat and death. But it has always been operative from the beginning. If God had not operated in grace He would have swept the human race away. He would have crushed Adam and Eve under His heel in awful judgment, for they had it coming.

But because God was a God of grace, He already had an eternity planned—the plan of grace, "the Lamb that was slain from the creation of the world" (Revelation 13:8). There was no embarrassment in the divine scheme; God didn't have to back up and say, "I'm sorry, but I have mixed things up here." He simply went right on.

Everybody receives in some degree God's grace: the lowest woman in the world; the most sinful, bloody man in the world; Judas; Hitler. If it hadn't been that God was gracious, they would have been cut off and slain, along with you and me and all the rest. I wonder if there's much difference in us sinners after all.

When a woman sweeps up a house, some of the dirt is black, some is gray, some is light-colored, but it is all dirt, and it all goes before the broom. And when God looks at humanity, He sees some that are morally light-colored, some that are morally dark, some that are morally speckled, but it is all dirt, and it all goes before the moral broom.

So the grace of God is operated toward everybody. But the saving grace of God is different. When the grace of God becomes operative through faith in Jesus Christ then there is the new birth. But the grace of God nevertheless holds back any judgment that would come until God in His kindness has given everyone a chance to repent.

Grace Is What God Is Like

Grace is God's goodness, the kindness of God's heart, the good will, the cordial benevolence. It is what God is like. God is like that all the time. You'll never run into a stratum in God that is hard. You'll always find God gracious, at all times and toward all peoples forever. You'll never run into any meanness in God, never any resentment or rancor or ill will, for there is none there. God has no ill will toward any being. God is a God of utter kindness and cordiality and good will and benevolence. And yet all of these work in perfect harmony with God's justice and God's judgment. I believe in hell and I believe in judgment. But I also believe that there are those whom God must reject because of their impenitence, yet there will be grace. God will still feel gracious toward all of His universe. He is God and He can't do anything else.

Grace is infinite, but I don't want you to strain to understand infinitude. I had the temerity to preach on infinitude a few times, and I got along all right—at least *I* got along all right. Let's try to measure it against ourselves, not against God. God never measures anything in Himself against anything else in Himself. That is, God never measures His grace against His justice or His mercy against His love. God is all one. But God measures His grace against our sin. "Grace . . . overflow[s] to the many," says Romans 5:15, "in accordance with the riches of God's grace" (Ephesians 1:7). And, says Romans 5 again, "But where sin increased, grace increased all the more" (5:20). God says "all the more," but God has no degrees. Man has degrees.

One of the worst things you can do is to give people IQ tests. When I was in the army I had an IQ test and I rated very high, and I have had a lifetime of trying to keep from remembering that and keeping humble before God. I think how I rated up in the top four percent in all of the army, and of course, you know what that does to a person. You have to keep humbling yourself, and God has to keep chastening you to keep you down.

But there's nothing in God that can compare itself with anything else in God. What God is, God is! When Scripture says grace "increased all the more," it means not that grace increases more than anything else in God but more than anything in us. No matter how much sin a man has done, literally and truly grace abounds unto that man.

Old John Bunyan wrote his life story and called it—I think it was one of the finest titles ever given to a book—*Grace Abounding Toward the Chief of Sinners*. Bunyan honestly believed that he was the man who had the least right to the grace of God. Grace abounded! For us who stand under the disapproval of God, who by sin lie under sentence of God's eternal, everlasting displeasure and banishment, grace is an incomprehensibly immense and overwhelming plenitude of kindness and goodness. If we could only remember it, we wouldn't have to be played with and entertained so much. If we could only remember the grace of God toward us who have nothing but demerit, we would be overwhelmed by this incomprehensibly immense attribute, so vast, so huge, that nobody can ever grasp it or hope to understand it.

Would God have put up with us this long if He had only a limited amount of grace? If He had only a limited amount of anything, He wouldn't be God. I shouldn't use the word *amount*, because *amount* means "a measure," and you can't measure God in any direction. God dwells in no dimension and can be measured in no way. Measures belong to human beings. Measures belong to the stars.

Distance is the way heavenly bodies account for the space they occupy and their relation to other heavenly bodies. The moon is 250,000 miles away. The sun is 93 million miles away, and all that sort of thing. But God never accounts to anybody for anything He is. God's immensity and His infinitude must mean that the grace of God must always be immeasurably full. We sing "Amazing Grace"—why, of course it's amazing! How can we comprehend the fullness of the grace of God?

How to Look at Grace

There are two ways to think about the grace of God: One is to look at yourself and see how sinful you were and say, "God's grace must be vast—it must be huge as space to forgive such a sinner as I am." That's one way and that's a good way—and probably that's the most popular way.

But there's another way to think of the grace of God. Think of it as the way God is—God being like God. And when God shows grace to a sinner He isn't being dramatic; He's acting like God. He'll never act any other way but like God. On the other hand, when that man whom justice has condemned turns his back on the grace of God in Christ and refuses to allow himself to be rescued, then the time comes when God must judge the man. And when God judges the man He acts like Himself in judging the man. When God shows love to the human race He acts like Himself. When God shows judgment to "the angels who did not keep their positions of authority but abandoned their own home" (Jude 6), He acts like Himself.

Always God acts in conformity with the fullness of His own wholly perfect, symmetrical nature. God always feels this overwhelming plentitude of goodness and He feels it in harmony with all His other attributes. There's no frustration in God. Everything that God is He is in complete harmony, and there is never any frustration in Him. But all this He bestows in His eternal Son.

A lot of people have talked about the goodness of God and then gotten sentimental about it and said, "God is too good to punish anybody," and so they have ruled out hell. But the man who has an adequate conception of God will not only believe in the love of God, but also in the holiness of God. He will not only believe in the mercy of God, but also in the justice of God. And when you see the everlasting God in His holy, perfect union, when you see the One God acting in judgment, you know that the man who chooses evil must never dwell in the presence of this holy God.

But a lot of people have gone too far and have written books and poetry that gets everybody believing that God is so kind and loving and gentle. God is so kind that infinity won't measure it. And God is so loving that He is immeasurably loving. But God is also holy and just.

Keep in mind that the grace of God comes only through Jesus Christ, and it is channeled only through Jesus Christ. The second Person of the Trinity opened the channel and grace flowed through. It flowed through from the day that Adam sinned all through Old Testament times, and it never flows any other way. So let's not write dreamy poetry about the goodness of our heavenly Father who is love—"love is God and God is love and love is all in all and all is God and everything will be OK." That's the summation of a lot of teaching these days. But it's false teaching.

Grace Is Released at the Cross

If I want to know this immeasurable grace, this overwhelming, astounding kindness of God, I have to step under the shadow of the cross. I must come where God releases grace. I must either look forward to it or I must look back at it. I must look one way or the other to that cross where Jesus died. Grace flowed out of His wounded side. The grace that flowed there saved Abel—and that same grace saves you. "No one comes to the Father except through me," said our Lord Jesus Christ (John 14:6). And Peter said, "There is no other name under heaven given to men by which we must be saved," except the name of Jesus Christ (Acts 4:12).

The reason for that is, of course, that Jesus Christ is God. Law could come by Moses and only law could come by Moses.

But grace came by Jesus Christ. And it came from the beginning. It could come only by Jesus Christ because there was no one else who was God who could die. No one else could take on Him flesh and still be the infinite God. And when Jesus walked around on earth and patted the heads of babies, forgave harlots and blessed mankind, He was simply God acting like God in a given situation. In everything that God does He acts like Himself.

CHAPTER 30

Joy Unspeakable

J t is amazing that we can claim to be followers of Christ and yet take so lightly the words of His servants. We could not act as we do if we took seriously the admonition of James the servant of God:

> My brothers, as believers in our glorious Lord Jesus Christ, don't show favoritism. Suppose a man comes into your meeting wearing a gold ring and fine clothes, and a poor man in shabby clothes also comes in. If you show special attention to the man wearing fine clothes and say, "Here's a good seat for you," but say to the poor man, "You stand there" or "Sit on the floor by my feet," have you not discriminated among yourselves and become judges with evil thoughts?

> Listen, my dear brothers: Has not God chosen those who are poor in the eyes of the world to be rich in faith and to inherit the kingdom he promised those who love him? (James 2:1-5)

Paul saw these things in another light than did those of whom James makes his complaint. "By the cross," he said, "I am crucified unto the world" (see Galatians 6:14). The cross where Jesus died became also the cross where His apostle died. The loss, the rejection, the shame, belong both to Christ and to all who in very truth are His. The cross that saves them also slays them, and anything short of this is a pseudo-faith and not true faith at all. But what are we to say when the great majority of our evangelical leaders walk not as crucified men but as those who accept the world at its own value—rejecting only its grosser elements? How can we face Him who was crucified and slain when we see His followers accepted and praised? Yet they preach the cross and protest loudly that they are true believers. Are there then two crosses? And did Paul mean one thing and they another? I fear that it is so, that there are two crosses, the old cross and the new.

Remembering my own deep imperfections I would think and speak with charity of all who take upon them the worthy Name by which we Christians are called. But if I see aright, the cross of popular evangelicalism is not the cross of the New Testament. It is, rather, a new bright ornament upon the bosom of self-assured and carnal Christianity whose hands are indeed the hands of Abel but whose voice is the voice of Cain. The old cross slew men; the new cross entertains them. The old cross condemned; the new cross amuses. The old cross destroyed confidence in the flesh; the new cross encourages it. The old cross brought tears and blood; the new cross brings laughter. The flesh, smiling and confident, preaches and sings about the cross; before the cross it bows and toward the cross it points with carefully staged histrionics—but upon that cross it will not die, and the reproach of that cross it stubbornly refuses to bear.

I well know how many smooth arguments can be marshalled in support of the new cross. Does not the new cross win converts and make many followers and so carry the advantage of numerical success? Should we not adjust ourselves to the changing times? Have we not heard the new slogan "New days, new ways"? And who but someone very old and very conservative would insist upon death as the appointed way to life? And who today is interested in a gloomy mysticism that would sentence its flesh to a cross and recommend self-effacing humility as a virtue actually to be practiced by modern Christians? These are the arguments, along with many more flippant still, which are brought forward to give an appearance of wisdom to the hollow and meaningless cross of popular Christianity.

Doubtless there are many whose eyes are open to the tragedy of our times, but why are they so silent when their testimony is so sorely needed? In the name of Christ men have made void the cross of Christ. "The noise of *them that* sing do I hear" (Exodus 32:18, KJV). Men have fashioned a golden cross with a graving tool, and before it they sit down to eat and drink and rise up to play. In their blindness they have substituted the work of their own hands for the working of God's power. Perhaps our greatest present need may be the coming of a prophet to dash the stones at the foot of the mountain and call the Church out to repentance or to judgment.

Before all who wish to follow Christ the way lies clear. It is the way of death unto life. Always life stands just beyond death and beckons the man who is sick of himself to come and know the life more abundant. But to reach the new life he must pass through the valley of the shadow of death, and I know that at the sound of those words many will turn back and follow Christ no more. But "to whom shall we go? You have the words of eternal life" (John 6:68).

It may be that there are some well-disposed followers who draw back because they cannot accept the morbidity which the idea of the cross seems to connote. They are lovers of the sun and find it too hard to think of living always in the shadows. They do not wish to dwell with death nor to live forever in an atmosphere of dying. And their instinct is sound. The Church has made altogether too much of deathbed scenes and churchyards and funerals. The musty smell of churches, the slow and solemn step of the minister, the subdued quiet of the worshipers and the fact that many enter a church only to pay their last respects to the dead all add up to the notion that religion is something to be dreaded and, like a major operation, suffered only because we are caught in a crisis. All this is not the religion of the cross; it is rather a gross parody on it. Churchyard Christianity, though not ever remotely related to the doctrine of the cross, may yet be partly to blame for the appearance of the new and jolly cross of today. Men crave life, but when they are told that life comes by the cross they cannot understand how it can be, for they have learned to associate with the cross such typical images as memorial plaques, dimly lit aisles and ivy. So they reject the true message of the cross and with that message they reject the only hope of life known to the sons of man.

The truth is that God has never planned that His children should live forever stretched upon a cross. Christ Himself endured His cross for only six hours. When the cross had done its work life entered and took over. "Therefore God exalted him to the highest place / and gave him the name that is above every name" (Philippians 2:9).

His joyful resurrection followed hard upon His joyless crucifixion. But the first had to come before the second. The life that halts short of the cross is but a fugitive and condemned thing, doomed at last to be lost beyond recovery. That life which goes to the cross and loses itself there to rise again with Christ is a divine and deathless treasure. Over it death hath no more dominion. Whoever refuses to bring his old life to the cross is but trying to cheat death, and no matter how hard we may struggle against it, he is nevertheless fated to lose his life at last. The man who takes his cross and follows Christ will soon find that his direction is *away* from the sepulcher. Death is behind him and a joyous and increasing life before. His days will be marked henceforth not by ecclesiastical gloom, the churchyard, the hollow tone, the black robe (which are all but the cerements* of a dead church), but by "joy unspeakable and full of glory" (1 Peter 1:8, KJV).

---

* cerement: a shroud used to wrap a dead body.

CHAPTER 31

Our Hope of Future Blessedness

od being God of infinite goodness must by the necessity of His nature will for each of His creatures the fullest measure of happiness consistent with its capacities and with the happiness of all other creatures.

Furthermore, being omniscient and omnipotent, God has the wisdom and power to achieve whatever He wills. The redemption which He provided for us through the incarnation, death and resurrection of His only Son guarantees eternal blessedness to all who through faith become beneficiaries of that redemption.

This the Church teaches her children to believe, and her teaching is more than hopeful thinking. It is founded upon the fullest and plainest revelations of the Old and New Testaments. That it accords with the most sacred yearnings of the human heart does not in any manner weaken it, but serves rather to confirm the truth of it, since the One who made the heart might be expected also to make provision for the fulfillment of its deepest longings.

While Christians believe this in a general way it is still difficult for them to visualize life as it will be in heaven, and it is especially hard for them to picture themselves as inheriting such bliss as the Scriptures describe. The reason for this is not hard to discover. The most godly Christian is the one who knows himself best, and no one who knows himself will believe that he deserves anything better than hell.

The man who knows himself least is likely to have cheerful if groundless confidence in his own moral worth. Such a man has less trouble believing that he will inherit an eternity of bliss because his concepts are only quasi-Christian, being influenced strongly by chimney-corner scripture and old wives tales. He thinks of heaven as being very much like California without the heat and the smog, and himself as inhabiting a splendiferous palace with all modern conveniences and wearing a heavily bejeweled crown. Throw in a few angels and you have the vulgar picture of the future life held by the devotees of popular Christianity.

This is the heaven that appears in the saccharin ballads of the guitar-twanging rockabilly gospellers that clutter up the religious scene today. That the whole thing is completely unrealistic and contrary to the laws of the moral universe seems to make no difference to anyone. As a pastor I have laid to rest the mortal remains of many a man whose future could not but be mighty uncertain but who before the funeral was over nevertheless managed to get title to a mansion just over the hilltop. I have steadfastly refused to utter any word that would add to the deception, but the emotional wattage of the singing was so high that the mourners went away vaguely believing that in spite of all they knew about the deceased everything would be all right some bright morning.

No one who has felt the weight of his own sin or heard from Calvary the Savior's mournful cry, "My God, my God, why have you forsaken me?" (Matthew 27:46) can ever allow his soul to rest on the feeble hope popular religion affords. He will—indeed he must—insist upon forgiveness and cleansing and the protection the vicarious death of Christ provides.

"God made him who had no sin to be sin for us, so that in him we might become the righteousness of God" (2 Corinthians 5:21). So wrote Paul, and Luther's great outburst of faith shows what this can mean in a human soul. "O Lord," cried Luther, "Thou art my righteousness, I am Thy sin."

Any valid hope of a state of blessedness beyond the incident of death must lie in the goodness of God and the work of atonement accomplished for us by Jesus Christ on the cross. The deep, deep love of God is the fountain out of which flows our future beatitude, and the grace of God in Christ is the channel by which it reaches us. The cross of Christ creates a moral situation where every attribute of God is on the side of the returning sinner. Even justice is on our side, for it is written, "If we confess our sins, he is faithful and just and will forgive us our sins and purify us from all unrighteousness" (1 John 1:9).

The true Christian may safely look forward to a future state that is as happy as perfect love wills it to be. Since love cannot desire for its object anything less than the fullest possible measure of enjoyment for the longest possible time, it is virtually beyond our power to conceive of a future as consistently delightful as that which Christ is preparing for us. And who is to say what is possible with God?

Appendix

The Brand of the Cross

About A.B. Simpson

The Brand of the Cross

by A.B. Simpson

Finally, let no one cause me trouble, for I bear on my body the marks of Jesus. (Galatians 6:17)

The word *marks* in this text is translated . . . "brand marks." The word describes a mark that has been branded into the flesh and suggests the idea of the cruel practice of certain nations in branding political offenders in the face with a badge of dishonor which never could be erased. The Greek word literally means "a stigma," and suggests a mark of reproach and shame. The Apostle [Paul] says that he bears in his body the branded scar which identifies him with Christ and His cross.

The kind of mark which he refers to is made plain by the verse almost immediately preceding. "May I never boast except in the cross of our Lord Jesus Christ, through which the world has been crucified to me, and I to the world" (6:14). It is the cross of Christ which is the object at once of His shame and His glory. Let us look first at the marks of the Lord Jesus and then at their reproduction in His followers.

The Cross Marks of Christ

He was always overshadowed by the cross which at last He bore on Calvary. His life was a life of humiliation and suffering from the manger to the tomb.

His birth was under a shadow of dishonor and shame. The shadow that fell upon the virgin mother could not be removed from her child, and even to this day only faith in a supernatural incarnation can explain away that reproach.

His childhood was overshadowed by sorrow. Soon after His birth, He was pressed by Herod with relentless hate. He spent His early childhood as an exile in the land of Egypt, which had always been associated in the history of His people as the house of bondage.

His early manhood was spent in toil and poverty and he was known all His later life as "the carpenter's son." A modern painter represents Him as under the shadow of the cross even in the early days at Nazareth; as He returns from a day of toil with arms outstretched with weariness, the setting sun flings the shadow of his figure across the pathway, suggestive of a dark cross.

His life was one of poverty and humiliation. He had nowhere to lay His head, and when He died His body was laid even in a borrowed tomb.

He was rejected and despised by the people among whom He labored. "He came to that which was his own, but his own did not receive him" (John 1:11). His work was, humanly speaking, a complete failure. When He left the world, He had but a handful of followers who had remained true to His teachings and person.

His very friends and companions were of the humblest class, rude fishermen and common people without culture and, indeed, often without the ability to appreciate their blessed Master. Coming from the society of heaven, how He must have felt the strange difference of these rude associates; and yet, never once did He complain or even intimate the difference.

The spirit of His life was ever chastened and humble. The veil of modesty covered all His acts and attitudes. He never boasted or vaunted Himself. "He will not quarrel or cry out; / no one will hear his voice in the streets" (Matthew 12:19) was the prophetic picture which He so literally fulfilled. He sought no splendid pageants, asked no earthly honors; and the only time that He did assume the prerogatives of a king, He rode upon the foal of an ass and entered Jerusalem in triumph as the King of meekness rather than of pride.

Perhaps the severest strain of all His life was the repression of Himself. Knowing that He was almighty and divine, He yet held back the exercise of His supernatural powers. Knowing that with one withering glance he could have stricken His enemies and laid them lifeless at His feet, He restrained His power. Knowing that He could have summoned all the angels of heaven to His defense, He surrendered Himself to His captors in helplessness and defenselessness. He even surrendered the exercise of His own will and drew from His heavenly Father the very grace and power which He needed from day to day, the same as any sinful man who lives by faith and prayer. "By myself I can do nothing" (John 5:30), He said. "Just as the living Father sent me and I live because of the Father, so the one who feeds on me will live because of me" (6:57). He took the same place of dependence that the humblest believer takes today and in all things lived a life of self-renunciation.

At last the climax came to the supreme trial of the judgment hall and the cruel cross. When He became obedient unto death, a death of shame and unparalleled humiliations, insults and agonies completed His life sacrifices for the salvation of His people. What words can ever describe, what tongue can ever tell the weight, the sharpness, the agony of that cruel cross, the fierceness of His fight with the powers of darkness and the depths of woe when even His Father's face was averted and He bore for us the hell that sin deserved.

After His resurrection, He still bore the marks of the cross. The few glimpses that we find of the risen Christ are all marked by the same touches of gentleness, self-abnegation and remembered suffering. The very evidences that He gave them that He was the same Jesus were the marks of the spear and the nails. And in His manifestations to them, especially in that memorable scene at Emmaus, we see the same gentle, unobtrusive Christ, walking with them by the way unrecognized, and then quietly vanishing out of their sight when at last they knew Him.

And even on the throne to which He has now ascended, the same cross marks still remain amid the glories of the heavenly world. John beheld Him as "a Lamb, looking as if it had been slain" (Revelation 5:6). The Christ of heaven still bears the old marks of the cross as His highest glory and His everlasting memorial. Such are the marks of the Lord Jesus. And all who claim to be His followers and His ministers may well imitate them. The men who claim to be His apostles and ambassadors, and who come to us with the sound of trumpets, the bluster of earthly pageants and the pompous and egotistical boastings of pride and vainglory, are false prophets and wretched counterfeits of the Christ of Calvary. They can deceive only the blind and ignorant dupes who know nothing of the real Christ.

These were the marks of the Master, and they will be worn by His servants, too.

The Cross Marks of the Christian

"No servant is greater than his master" (John 13:16). The tests of the Master must be applied to His followers. We may not preach a crucified Savior without being also crucified men and women. It is not enough to wear an ornamental cross as a pretty decoration. The cross that Paul speaks about was burned into his very flesh, was branded into his being, and only the Holy Spirit can burn the true cross into our innermost life.

We are saved by identification with Christ in His death. We are justified because we have already died with Him and have thus been made free from sin. God does not whitewash people when He saves them. He has really visited their sins upon their great Substitute, the Lord Jesus Christ. Every believer was counted as in Him when He died, and so His death is our death. It puts us in the same position before the law of the supreme Judge as if we had already been executed and punished for our own guilt, as if the judgment for us was already past. Therefore, it is true of every believer, "whoever hears my word and believes him who sent me has eternal life and will not be condemned; he has crossed over from death to life" (5:24). The cross, therefore, is the very standpoint of the believer's salvation, and we shall never cease to echo the song of heaven: "Worthy is the Lamb, who was slain, / to receive . . . honor and glory and praise!" (Revelation 5:12).

We are sanctified by dying with Christ to sin. When He hung on Calvary, He not only made a settlement for our sinful self, by faith we reckon ourselves as actually crucified with Him there to the whole life of sin. It is our privilege, therefore, to identify ourselves with Christ in His death so fully that we may lay over our sinful nature upon Him and utterly die to it, and then receive from Him a life all new, divine and pure. Henceforth we may say, "I no longer live, but Christ lives in me" (Galatians 2:20). Sanctification is not the cleansing of the old life, but the crucifying of that life and substituting for it the very life of Christ Himself, the holy and perfect One.

We must keep sanctified by dead reckoning. And dead reckoning is just the reckoning of ourselves as "dead to sin but alive to God in Christ Jesus" (Romans 6:11). This is not merely a feeling or experience, but a counting upon Him as life and drawing from Him as breath from the air around us.

Our spiritual life is perfected by the constant recognition of the cross and by our unceasing application of it to all our life and being. We must live by the cross and must pass from death to death and life to life by constant fellowship with His sufferings and conformity unto His death, until at last we shall "attain to the resurrection from the dead" (Philippians 3:11).

Now this principle of death and resurrection underlies all nature as well as the Bible. The autumn leaves with their rich crimson are just a parable of nature's dying to make way for the resurrection of the coming spring. Pick up an acorn in the forest, and in its heart, as you break the shell, you will find a crimson hairline as the cross mark of its hidden life. When it bursts through the ground in the spring, the first opening leaf is red, the color of the cross, and when the leaf dies and falls in autumn, it wraps itself in the same crimson hue.

But all this is but a stepping-stone of the life that follows. Look at the structure and growth of a flower. First, the calyx or flower cup tightly claps the enfolding petals, refusing to let go. But gradually these fingers relax, these folds unclasp and the petals burst open in all their fragrance and beauty. But still the calyx holds them tightly as if it would never let go, but hour by hour, as the flower-life advances, those petals have to be relinquished from the grasp; and in a little while the blossom floats away on the summer winds and seems to perish. "The flowers fall" (Isaiah 40:7), the beauty of nature dies. But observe that after death comes a richer life. Behind the flower you will notice a seed pod. It also is held for a time by the grasp of another cup. But as the seeds ripen, even they must let go this grasp, and gradually the seed pod relaxes and at length bursts open and the seeds are scattered and sink into the ground and die. But from the buried seed comes forth a new resurrection of plants and trees and flowers and fruits. The whole process is one of dying and living, one life giving place to a higher, and all moving steadily on to the reproduction of the plant and the stage of fruit bearing.

So marked is this principle in the natural world that botanists tell us that when a flower gives too much attention to the blossom and develops into a double flower, which is the most beautiful form of the blossom, it becomes barren and fruitless. Nature puts its ban upon self life even in a flower. It must die and pass away if it would bear much fruit. A beautiful double petunia is no good; but a single-petalled blossom has in it the life of another generation. And so our spiritual life must pass down to deeper deaths and on and up to the higher experiences of life, or we shall lose even what we have. We cannot cling to the sweetest spiritual experiences, the fondest object of our highest joy, without ceasing to grow and ceasing to bear that fruit which is the very nature of our salvation.

The Principle of Death in Our Deeper Life

We must learn not only to give up our wrongs but even our rights. It is little that we should turn from sin; if we are to follow Christ and His consecration, we must turn from the things that are not sinful and learn the great lesson of self-renunciation even in rightful things. The everlasting ideal is He, in the form of God, who thought it not a thing to be eagerly grasped that He should be equal with God, but emptied Himself and became obedient unto death, even the death of the cross (see Philippians 2:6–8). There are many things which are not wrong for you to keep and to hold as your own, but in keeping them, He would lose and you would lose much more.

We have the cross mark upon our affections and friendships. Thus Abraham gave up his Isaac and received him back with a new touch of love as God's Isaac. We shall find that most of the lives that counted much for God had somewhere in them a great renunciation, where the dearest idol was laid upon Moriah's altar* and from that hour there was new fruit and power.

Our prayers must often have the mark of the cross upon them. We ask and we receive the promise and assurance of the answer; and then we must often see that answer apparently buried and forgotten, and long after come forth, to our amazement and surprise, multiplied with blessings that have grown out of the very delay and seeming denial.

So the life of our body which we may claim from Him must be marked with the cross. It is only after the strength of nature

---

* Moriah's altar: a reference to the hill Abraham climbed to offer up his son Isaac to God (see Genesis 22:2).

fails us that the strength of God can come in. Even then the answer is sometimes not given until we have first surrendered it to Him and have been willing to give up even life itself and have learned to seek the Blesser rather than the blessing. Then God often reveals Himself to us as a Healer, as He could not do until we were wholly abandoned to His will.

Our religious experiences must have the mark of the cross upon them. We must not cling even to our peace and joy and spiritual comfort. Sometimes, the flower must fade that the fruit may be more abundant and that we may learn to walk by faith and not by sight.

Our service for God often must be buried before it can bring forth much fruit. And so God sometimes calls us to a work and makes it appear to fail in its early stages, until we cry in discouragement, "I have labored in vain, I have spent my strength for nought." Then it comes forth phoenixlike* from the flames and blossoms and buds until it fills the face of the world with fruit. So God writes the mark of the cross on everything, until, by and by, the very grave may be the passport to a better resurrection and death will be swallowed up in victory. In fact, we believe that the universe itself has yet to pass through its dissolution and come forth in the glory of a final resurrection so that the marks of the Lord Jesus may, at last, be written upon the very earth and heaven, and so that the universe to its furthest bound may reecho the great redemption song: "Worthy is the Lamb that was slain."

Beloved, have you the marks of the Lord Jesus? These sacrifices to which He sometimes calls us are just great investments that He is asking us to make and that He will refund to us with accumulated interest in the age to come.

Good Richard Cecil once asked his little daughter, as she sat upon his knee with a cluster of pretty glass beads around her neck, if she truly loved him, and if she loved him enough to

---

* Phoenix: a legendary bird that lived 500 years, burned itself to ashes on a pyre and then emerged fresh and young again.

take those beads and fling them into the fire. She looked in his face with wonder and grief; she could hardly believe that he meant such sacrifice. But his steady gaze convinced her that he was in earnest; and with trembling, reluctant steps she tottered to the grate, and clinging to them with reluctant fingers, at last dropped them into the fire, and then flinging herself into his arms, she sobbed herself to stillness in the bewilderment and perplexity of her renunciation. He let her learn her lesson fully, but a few days later, on her birthday, she found upon her dressing case a little package, and on opening it she found inside a cluster of real pearls strung upon a necklace and bearing her name with her father's love. She had scarcely time to grasp the beautiful present as she flew to his presence and throwing herself in his arms, she said, "Oh, Papa, I am so sorry that I did not understand."

Some day, beloved, in His arms, you will understand. He does not always explain it now. He lets the cross have all its sharpness. He lets the weary years go by; but oh, some day we will understand and be so glad that we were permitted to bear with Him and for Him the "brand marks of the Lord Jesus."

From *The Cross of Christ*
© 1994 by Zur Ltd.

About A.B. Simpson

Albert Benjamin Simpson was born on Prince Edward Island in 1843. A major figure in American evangelicalism at the close of the nineteenth century, he founded The Christian and Missionary Alliance movement. A prolific communicator, Simpson established a publishing house, edited a weekly missions magazine, wrote over 100 books, pastored key churches, launched social ministries, founded the first Bible college in the United States and penned dozens of hymns and gospel songs. Of him, Dwight L. Moody said, "No man gets at my heart like that man." C.I. Scofield noted that Simpson "was foremost in power to reach the depths of the human soul," and A.W. Tozer declared that in Simpson's mouth "doctrine became warm and living." Simpson died in 1919, leaving a vision that continues to expand around the globe.

KEY TO ORIGINAL SOURCES

The individual chapter selections in this book were compiled from the following books written by A.W. Tozer and published by WingSpread Publishers.

Chapter	Original Source
1	*The Root of the Righteous*
2	*The Attributes of God* (excerpted from the chapter "God's Justice")
3	*The Warfare of the Spirit*
4	*This World: Playground or Battleground?*
5	*Who Put Jesus on the Cross?* (excerpted from "Will You Allow God to Reproduce Christ's Likeness in You?")
6	*Man: The Dwelling Place of God*
7	*I Talk Back to the Devil* (excerpted from "Dark, Dark Night of the Soul!")
8	*Of God and Men*
9	*That Incredible Christian* (see "Chastisement and Cross Carrying Not the Same")
10	*Christ the Eternal Son* (excerpted from "The Divine Intention")
11	*Of God and Men*
12	*Tragedy in the Church* (excerpted from "The Presence of Christ: Meaning of the Communion")
13	*Man: The Dwelling Place of God*
14	*The Size of the Soul*
15	*The Root of the Righteous*
16	*The Early Tozer: A Word in Season*
17	*Success and the Christian* (excerpted from "Formula for Spiritual Success")
18	*I Talk Back to the Devil* (excerpted from "God Heard Elijah Because Elijah Heard God!")
19	*Of God and Men*

Titles by A.W. Tozer available through your local Christian bookstore or on the Web at www.echurchdepot.com:

Titles by A.B. Simpson available
through your local Christian bookstore
or on the Web at www.echurchdepot.com:

The Best of A.B. Simpson

Christ in the Bible Commentary
  (6 volumes)

Christ in the Tabernacle

Christ in You (formerly *The
  Christ-Life* and *The Christ-Life
  and The Self-Life*)

The Christ of the Forty Days

The Cross of Christ

Danger Lines in the Deeper Life

Days of Heaven on Earth

Divine Emblems

The Fourfold Gospel

The Gospel of Healing

Healing: Three Great Classics
  (Includes *The Gospel of Healing*)

The Holy Spirit

In Step with the Spirit (formerly
  Gentle Love of the Holy Spirit
  and *Walking in the Spirit*)

The Land of Promise

A Larger Christian Life

The Life of Prayer

The Lord for the Body

Loving as Jesus Loves

Missionary Messages

The Names of Jesus

*Portraits of a Spirit-Filled
  Personality*

Practical Christianity

The Quotable Simpson

Seeing the Invisible

Serving the King

The Spirit-Filled Church in Action

The Supernatural

Walking in Love

When God Steps In

When the Comforter Came

Wholly Sanctified

The Word Made Flesh